The Mistress's Daughter

Also by A.M. Homes

The Mistress's Daughter

A.M. HOMES

VIKING

VIKING
Published by the Penguin Group
Penguin Group (USA) Inc., 375 Hudson Street,
New York, New York 10014, U.S.A.
Penguin Group (Canada), 90 Eglinton Avenue East, Suite 700,
Toronto, Ontario, Canada M4P 2Y3
(a division of Pearson Penguin Canada Inc.)
Penguin Books Ltd, 80 Strand, London WC2R 0RL, England
Penguin Ireland, 25 St. Stephen's Green, Dublin 2, Ireland
(a division of Penguin Books Ltd)
Penguin Books Australia Ltd, 250 Camberwell Road, Camberwell,
Victoria 3124, Australia
(a division of Pearson Australia Group Pty Ltd)
Penguin Books India Pvt Ltd, 11 Community Centre, Panchsheel Park,
New Delhi – 110 017, India
Penguin Group (NZ), 67 Apollo Drive, Mairangi Bay, Auckland 1311,
New Zealand (a division of Pearson New Zealand Ltd.)
Penguin Books (South Africa) (Pty) Ltd, 24 Sturdee Avenue,
Rosebank, Johannesburg 2196, South Africa

Penguin Books Ltd, Registered Offices:
80 Strand, London WC2R 0RL, England

First published in 2007 by Viking Penguin,
a member of Penguin Group (USA) Inc.

10 9 8 7 6 5 4 3 2 1

Copyright © A.M. Homes, 2007
All rights reserved

ISBN 0-670-03838-5

Printed in the United States of America
Set in Janson Text
Designed by Spring Hoteling

B
Homes, A. M.
HOM

In memory of Jewel Rosenberg and
in honor of Juliet Spencer Homes

There are two ways to live your life—one is as though nothing is a miracle, the other is as though everything is a miracle.

ALBERT EINSTEIN

Contents

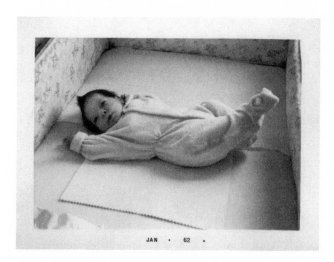

JAN · 62 ·

A.M. Homes

Book One

Phyllis and Joe Homes

Bruce Homes

A.M. and Jon Homes

The Mistress's Daughter

I remember their insistence that I come into the living room and sit down and how the dark room seemed suddenly threatening, how I stood in the kitchen doorway holding a jelly doughnut and how I never eat jelly doughnuts.

I remember not knowing; first thinking something was very wrong, assuming it was death—someone had died.

And then I remember knowing.

Christmas 1992, I go home to Washington, D.C., to visit my family. The night I arrive, just after dinner, my mother says, "Come into the living room. Sit down. We have something to tell you." Her tone makes me nervous. My parents are not formal people—no one sits in the living room. I am standing in the kitchen. The dog is looking up at me.

"Come into the living room. Sit down," my mother says.

"Why?"

"There's something we need to talk to you about."

"What?"

"Come and we'll tell you."

"Tell me now, from here."

"Come and we'll tell you."

"Tell me now, from here."

"Come," she says, patting the cushion next to her.

"Who died?" I say, terrified.

"No one died. Everyone's fine."

"Then what is it?"

They are silent.

"Is it about me?"

"Yes, it's you. We've had a phone call. Someone is looking for you."

After a lifetime spent in a virtual witness-protection program, I've been exposed. I get up knowing one thing about myself: I am the mistress's daughter. My birth mother was young and unmarried, my father older and married, with a family of his own. When I was born, in

December of 1961, a lawyer called my adoptive parents and said, "Your package has arrived and it's wrapped in pink ribbons."

My mother starts to cry. "You don't have to do anything about it, you can just let it go," she says, trying to relieve me of the burden. "But the lawyer said he'd be happy to talk with you. He couldn't have been nicer."

"Tell me again—what happened?"

Details, minutiae, as though the facts, the call-and-response of questions asked and answered, will make sense of it, will give it order, shape, and the thing it lacks most—logic.

"About two weeks ago we got a phone call. It was Stanley Frosh, the lawyer who took care of the adoption, calling to say that he'd gotten a call from a woman who told him that if you wanted to contact her, she'd be willing to hear from you."

"What does that mean, 'willing to hear from you'? Does she *want* to talk to me?"

"I don't know," my mother says.

"What did Frosh say?"

"He couldn't have been nicer. He said that he'd had this call—the day before your birthday—and he wasn't sure what we would want to do with the information, but he thought we should have it. Would you like to know her name?"

"No," I say.

"We debated about whether or not to even tell you," my father says.

"You debated? How could you not tell me? It's not your information. What if you hadn't told me and something happened to you and then I found out later?"

"But we are telling you," my mother says. "Mr. Frosh says you can call him at any time." She offers Frosh as though talking to him will do something—like fix it.

"This happened two weeks ago and you're just telling me now?"

"We wanted to wait until you were home."

"Why did Frosh call you? Why didn't he call me directly?" I was thirty-one years old, an adult, and still they were treating me like an infant who needed protection.

"Damn her," my mother says. "It's a lot of nerve."

This was my mother's nightmare; she'd always been afraid that someone would come and take me away. I'd grown up knowing that was her fear, knowing in part it had nothing to do with my being taken away, but with her first child, her son, having died just before I was born. I grew up feeling that on some very basic level my mother would never let herself get attached again. I grew up with the sensation of being kept at a distance. I grew up furious. I feared that there was something about me, some defect of birth that made me repulsive, unlovable.

My mother came to me. She wanted to hug me. She wanted me to comfort her.

I didn't want to hug her. I didn't want to touch anyone. "Is Frosh sure she is who she says she is?"

"What do you mean?" my father asked.

"Is he sure she's the right woman?"

"I think he's fairly certain it's her," my father said.

The fragile, fragmented narrative, the thin line of story, the plot of my life, has been abruptly recast. I am dealing with the divide between sociology and biology: the chemical necklace of DNA that wraps around the neck sometimes like a beautiful ornament—our birthright, our history—and other times like a choke chain.

I have often felt the difference between who I arrived as and who I've become; layer upon layer piling up until it feels as though I am coated with a bad veneer, the cheap paneling of a suburban recreation room.

As a child, I was obsessed by the *World Book Encyclopedia*, the acetate anatomy pages, where you could build a person, folding in the skeleton, the veins, the muscles, layer upon layer, until it all came together.

For thirty-one years I have known that I came from somewhere else, started as someone else. There have been times when I have been relieved by the fact that I am not *of* my parents, that I am freed from their biology; and that is followed by an enormous sensation of otherness, the pain of how alone I feel.

"Who else knows?"

"We told Jon," my father says. Jon, my older brother, their son.

"Why did you tell him? It wasn't yours to tell."

"We're not telling Grandma," my mother says.

This is the first important thing they've elected not to tell her—she is too old, too confused to be of help to them. She might do something with it in her head, conflate the information with other information, make it into something entirely different.

"Think of how I feel," my mother says. "I can't even tell my own mother. I can't get any comfort from her. It's awful."

My mother and I sit in silence.

"Should we not have told you?" my mother asks.

"No," I say, resigned. "You had to tell me. It wasn't a choice. It's my life, I have to deal with it."

"Mr. Frosh says you can call him anytime," she repeats.

"Where does she live?"

"New Jersey."

In my dreams, my birth mother is a goddess, the queen of queens, the CEO, the CFO, and the COO. Movie-star

beautiful, incredibly competent, she can take care of anyone and anything. She has made a fabulous life for herself,
as ruler of the world, except for one missing link—*me*.

I say good night and drift off into the spin of the story, the
myth of my beginning.

My adoptive mother and father didn't marry until my
father was forty. My mother, eight years younger, had a
son, Bruce, from a previous marriage who had been born
with severe kidney problems. He lived to be nine and died
six months before I was born. Together my mother and father had Jon—during his birth my mother's uterus rup-
tured, and both she and Jon nearly died. An emergency
hysterectomy was performed and my mother was unable
to have more children.

"It was lucky any of us survived," she said. "We always
wanted more. We wanted three children. We wanted a little girl."

When I was young and used to ask where I came from,
my mother would tell me that I was from the Jewish Social
Service Agency. When I was a teenager, my therapist often
asked me, "Don't you think it's odd that an agency would
give a baby to a family where another child had died just
six months before—to a family still in mourning?" I
shrugged. It seemed like both a good idea and a really bad
one. I always felt that my role in the family was to heal

things, to make everything all right—to replace a dead boy. I grew up doused in grief. From day one, on a cellular level, I was perpetually in mourning.

There is folklore, there are the myths, there are facts, and there are the questions that go unanswered.

If my parents wanted more children, why did they build a house with only three bedrooms—who was going to share? I assumed that they knew Bruce was going to die. They may have wanted three children, but they planned for two.

When I asked my mother why an agency would give them an infant so soon after a child had died, she said nothing. And then when I was twenty, on a cold winter afternoon, I pressed her for more information, details. I would do this at weak moments, special occasions such as Bruce's birthday, the anniversary of his death, or my birthday—times when she seemed vulnerable, when I sensed a crack in the surface. Where did I come from? Not from an agency, but through a lawyer; it was a private adoption.

"We put our name on agency lists but there were no babies available. We were told that the best thing to do was ask around, to let people know that we were looking for a baby."

Each earthquake of identity, each shift in the architecture of the precarious frame that I'd built for myself, threw me. How much was still being kept from me and how much had been forgotten, or lost with the subtle erasure, the natural revision of time?

I asked again. "Where did I come from?"

"We told everyone that we were looking for a baby and then one day we heard of a baby that was going to be born, and that was you."

"How did you hear about me?"

"Through a friend. Remember my friend Lorraine?" She mentioned the name of someone I met once, long ago. Lorraine knew another couple that also wanted to adopt a baby, but it turned out that in a roundabout way they knew who the mother was—this was told to me as though it explained something, as though knowing who the mother was made everything null and void, not because there was something wrong with the mother, but because there was something wrong with knowing.

As an adult I asked my mother if she would call Lorraine, if she would ask Lorraine to call the people who in a roundabout way knew who my mother was and ask them, who was she? My mother said no. She said, what if the couple has other children that don't know they're adopted?

What does that have to do with me? And how incredibly screwed up that someone wouldn't have told their children that they were adopted.

My mother finally called Lorraine—who said, "Let it go." She claimed to know nothing. Who was she protecting? What was she hiding?

My mother remembered something about real estate, something about a name, but she didn't remember enough. Why didn't she remember? It would seem like the kind of thing you wouldn't forget.

"I didn't want to remember. I didn't want to know anything. I felt I had to protect you. The less I knew, the better. I was afraid she would come back and try to take you away."

"Okay, back to the beginning—you heard of a baby who was going to be born, and then what?"

"And then PopPop's lawyer was able to get in touch with the woman and they met and he called us and said, she's wonderful, she's healthy, except for some problems with her teeth—I think she hadn't had good dental care. We set up a post office box and some letters were exchanged, and then we waited for you to be born."

"What did the letters say?"

"I don't remember." Everything is prefaced with "I don't remember."

I lean in and the subtle pressure causes some slight discharge of information. "Just some basic information about her background, about her health, about how the pregnancy was going. She was young, she wasn't married. I think that the father was married. One of them was Jewish; the other, I think, may have been Catholic. She cared about you very much, she wanted what was best for you and knew she couldn't take care of you herself. She wanted you to go to a very special home—a Jewish home. It was important to her to know that you went somewhere where you'd be loved. She wanted you to have all the opportunity in the world. I think she may have been living in northern Virginia."

"What happened to the letters?" I imagine a precious short stack of delicate letters tied in a ribbon and buried at the back of a drawer deep in my mother's dresser.

My mother pauses, looks up and off to the side, as if searching her memory. "I think there was even another letter after you were born."

"Where are the letters?"

"I think they were destroyed," my mother says.

"Didn't it occur to you that I might want them, that they might be all I ever had?"

"We were told to be very careful. I didn't save anything. We were told not to. No evidence, no reminders."

"Who told you?"

"The lawyer."

I didn't believe her. It was her choice. My mother didn't want me to be adopted. She wanted me to be hers. She was afraid of anything that challenged that.

"And then what?"

"We waited. And on December 18, 1961, we got a phone call from the lawyer saying, 'Your package has arrived, it's wrapped in pink ribbons and it has ten fingers and ten toes.' We called Dr. Ross, our pediatrician, and he went down to the hospital, took a look at you, and called us. 'She's perfect,' he said."

"What else?"

"Three days later we went to pick you up."

I met my parents for the first time in a car parked around the corner from the hospital. They sat parked on a street in downtown Washington in the middle of a snowstorm, waiting for me to be delivered to them. They brought clothing to dress me, to disguise me, to begin to make me their own. This undercover pickup and delivery was made by a friend who purposely dressed in ratty old clothes—her costume designed not to attract attention, not to give information; this is another detail I didn't know until I was in my twenties. My parents sat in the car, worrying, while the neighbor went into the hospital to collect me. This was a secret mission, something could go wrong. *She*—the mother—could change her mind. They sat waiting, and then the neighbor was there walking through the snow with a bundle in her arms. She handed me to my mother, and my parents brought me home, mission accomplished.

I have only the home movie version in my head. A big old-fashioned 1961 car. Downtown Washington. Snow. Nervousness. Excitement.

The story goes that my brother, Jon, so proud, so thrilled that the new baby was coming home, stood out in the driveway with a sign that he and my grandmother had

made—"Welcome Home Baby Sister." My arrival has always been described as if it were some magical moment, as
if a fairy had waved a wand that pronounced the household
cured, leaving me there, like a token, a good luck charm to
fix everything, to lift a mother and father from their grief.

I was carried down the hall and laid out on the big bed
in my parents' room. Neighbors, the aunts and uncles, all
came to look at me; a prize—the most beautiful baby
they'd ever seen. My hair was thick and black and stood up
like a rocket ship, my eyes were bright blue. "Your cheeks
were luscious and pink—we ate you up. You were perfect."

Think of the differences in anticipation; with a non-
adopted baby, members of the family would have visited
the hospital. They would have seen me with my mother,
or visited me in the nursery, picking me out from the police lineup of bassinets.

But here it begins with a phone call: Your package has
arrived and is wrapped in pink ribbons. The trusted pediatrician dispatched to the hospital to make an evaluation of
the merchandise—think of movies where the drug dealer
samples the stuff before turning over the cash. There is
something inescapably sordid about the way the story unfolds. I was adopted, purchased, ordered, and picked up
like a cake from a bakery.

When I was twenty my mother confessed that the
"friend" who collected me was the next-door neighbor. I
couldn't believe that all these years, I had lived next door

to someone who had seen my mother, who had actually met her face-to-face.

I dialed the neighbor's house. "So?" I said. "You saw my mother?" The neighbor was cautious. "I hope you're not going to do something about this," she said. "I hope you're not going to pursue it." It amazed me that this was the reaction. What was her fear? That I would disrupt my family, the woman's family, that I would wreak havoc? What about me, my life, the deep chaos that had been my existence?

"What did she look like?"

"She was beautiful. She had on a tweed suit and I couldn't believe that she had just had a baby. She didn't look pregnant at all. She was thin. And her hair was up in a bun."

I pictured Audrey Hepburn.

"Did she look like me?"

I can't remember what the neighbor said. I was suffering the deafness that comes in moments of great importance.

"I wore bad clothing," the neighbor was telling me. "I disguised myself. I didn't want her to know anything. And she too was very concerned about anyone knowing who she was."

The amount of mystery that surrounded the proceedings was enormous, everything was subtext and secrecy.

Beneath the intrigue was the element of shame that no one ever talked about.

" 'If you ever see me, don't acknowledge me,' the woman said. Meaning that if I ever saw her at a party or around town, I should pretend that I didn't know her," the neighbor told me.

"Did you ever see her again?"

"No, I never saw her again."

"If you ever see me, don't acknowledge me." The one line of dialogue, the only direct quote.

In the morning my mother comes into my room with a scrap of paper; she sits at the edge of my bed and asks me again, "Do you want the name?"

I don't answer. Even if I want it, I can't say so—it feels like a betrayal.

"It's the same name as a friend of yours," she says, as if she were trying to warm it up, to detoxify it, to make it somehow more palatable. "I think she has a brother, a lawyer who lives in the area—Frosh recognized the name."

"You can just leave it on the desk," I say. Her name is Ellen. Ellen Ballman. It sounds like a fake name. Ball-man. What is she like? What does she do? Is she smart?

I once met an adopted woman whose mother had come back and found her. The mother was a photographer who traveled a lot. She was lovely, warm, respectful. She said, "I just want you to know I'm here if you need me."

Ellen has a brother who lives in the area, my mother had said. I look up the brother's address. I go for a ride. I am trying it on—the concept of biological family. His house is on my regular route. As a habit, I drive to think, I drive the way other people jog. I have a regular routine, landmarks. I have been riding up and down this road for years, fixated on the roll of the hills, the long driveways— how strange that my uncle's house is just a left turn away.

White brick, lots of cars, a basketball hoop in the driveway—a sore point. As a kid the thing I wanted most was a hoop. A hundred times a year I asked for one—and my parents, entirely unathletic, would say no. A hoop would ruin the aesthetic integrity of the house. I played next door, I played up the street, I played until inevitably someone would stick their head out a window and suggest I go home for dinner.

I park outside the uncle's house; this is the first time I've been within feet of someone biologically connected to me. I sit and imagine them inside, the uncle and his sons, my cousins. The Christmas decorations are up. I see their tree through the window. I imagine this as a joyous, prosperous place. I imagine they are somehow better than me—I drive away.

I call a private investigator, the friend of a friend—also adopted. I give her what little information I have.

"Give me a couple of hours," she says.

I am a spy, a hunter, hot on the trail. I have no idea what I'm doing except that I want information, something to go on before I proceed. I don't want any more surprises. The P.I. calls me back.

"The woman you're looking for doesn't have a phone listed in her name in New Jersey. And she doesn't have a local driver's license, but she does own a home in the Washington area."

The P.I. gives me the address. I get back in the car. It's nearby, very nearby. Did she really live that close? Has she lived there all along? Might I have seen her somewhere without knowing it—in a shopping mall, or a restaurant? I circle the house. It looks empty. I park, knock on a neighbor's door—asking questions, talking to strangers. What is a stranger? Who is a stranger? She could well be my mother.

"Do you know what happened to the folks next door? Moved? Any idea where to?" Dead end.

I go to the library of my childhood, of book reports and science projects. I look things up. I am always looking things up. I get a map of the town in New Jersey where she lives, I find her street. I look in phone books, call information. Nothing. Why is she not listed? Does she live with someone? Does she have another name? Is she a liar? An outlaw?

*   *   *

I call Frosh, the lawyer. "A letter. I'd like a letter," I say. "I want information—where she grew up, how educated she is, what she does for a living, what the family medical history is, and what the circumstances of my adoption were."

I am asking for the story of my life. There is an urgency to my request; I feel as if I should hurry and ask everything I want to know. As suddenly as she has arrived, she could be gone again.

As soon as I hang up, I start waiting for the letter.

Ten days later, her letter arrives with no fanfare. The postman doesn't come running down the street, screaming, "It's here, it's here! Your identity has arrived." It comes in an envelope from the lawyer's office with a scrawled note from the lawyer apologizing for not having got it to me sooner. It's clear that the letter has been opened, presumably read. Why? Is nothing private? I am annoyed but don't say anything. I don't feel I have the right. It's one of the pathological complications of adoption—adoptees don't really have rights, their lives are about supporting the secrets, the needs and desires of others.

The letter is typed on her stationery, simple small gray sheets of paper, her name embossed across the top. Her language is oddly formal, less than artful, grammatically flawed. I read it simultaneously fast and slow, wanting to take it in, unable to take it in. I read it and then read it again. What is she telling me?

> . . . . at the time I was carrying this little girl it was not proper for a girl to have a child out of wedlock. This was probably the most difficult decision of my entire life to make. I was 22 years old and very naive. I was raised very sheltered and very strict by my mother.
>
> I remember being in the hospital with her and dressing her the day we both left the hospital. I have never forgotten the beautiful black hair and the blue eyes and the little dimples in her face. As I left the hospital with the lady who was picking up the little girl, I can still see myself in the taxi and her asking me to give her the baby. I did not want to give her the child, however, I did realize, I did not have the wear-with-all to take care of her myself. Yes, I have always loved this little girl and been tortured every December of my life from the day she was born that I did not have her with me.

She writes that watching television shows like Oprah and Maury gave her the courage and the confidence to come forward. She lists the facts of where she was born, what street she lived on as a child, how she grew up. She tells the names of her parents and when they died. She says how tall she is and how much she weighs.

She writes of never forgetting.

Each bit of information swims through me, takes root, digging in. There are no filters, there are no screens. I have no protection from this.

She closes her letter by saying, "I have never married, I have always felt guilty about giving this little girl away."

I am that little girl.

I call the lawyer and ask for another letter, with more information, a medical history, a more detailed explanation of what happened, what she's been doing since, and a photograph of her.

A day later, in a panic, I call the lawyer back. "Oh," I say. "Oh, I forgot. Could you ask her who the father is?" Not my father, but *the* father."

"Okay," he says. "Okay. I'll put it on the list."

Within days, a second letter arrives, again having been opened.

I suppose now, I should tell you about Norman Hecht. This is difficult for me because to me it is turning back the hands of time. I went to work for Norman at the Princess Shop in downtown Washington D.C. I was 15 years old. I worked for him on Thursday night and on Saturdays. During the summer, I worked fulltime. Norman as you know was much older than I. He was very nice to me. This relationship started very innocently. He would offer to drive me home and we would talk about many things on the way. Then one day while we were working he asked me if I would like to go to dinner with him. This was the beginning. At age 17, he called my mother and asked if he could marry me. My mother said, "she is too young." Hung up the telephone, turned to me and said, I do not want you to see this man ever again. At this time, I was in love and nothing she said would stop me. I have always been a very determined person. Stubborn if you will. This is me. Norman is married at that time and promises to get a divorce and marry me. This was not my idea but his. Time goes on, I become pregnant with the young lady. He thinks I should go to Florida. He will buy a house for us both. About three months later, I am very unhappy. I return to Washington. Norman and I start to have disagreements. During the last three months of the pregnancy I stayed with my mother in Virginia where her home was. Shortly before the baby was born, Norman again said he would marry me. He asked if he could come and pick me up and take me to buy things for the baby. I told him no. I did not call him when the baby was born.

Norman to the best of my knowledge lives in Potomac, Md. He has four children. All of his children were born prior to the birth of our child. He was an All American Football Player. To the best of my knowledge his father was Jewish, his mother, Irish. I knew only his mother. She was a little chubby lady. Very kind and very nice to me.

You asked about my general health. I periodically do have a problem with bronchitis. This is treated with medicine. Damp weather is not for me. I do take pills for high blood pressure. Other than that, I am fine. I am nearsighted and do have soft teeth. Both inherited, my eyes from my father, my teeth from my mother.

She ends her second letter, ". . . I have a great fear of being disappointed with what I am now doing."

Later, she will tell me that Frosh, reading the letter, recognized the father's name and called her saying that if she was going to give the father's name, she'd better let the father know what she was doing. She will tell me that she called my father and that he was shocked to hear from her, horrified at what she was doing, and told her that watching Oprah and Maury was beneath her.

Frosh is driving me crazy with his tinkering. It is an intrusion and interruption of the events—whose side is he on, what is he looking for, who is he trying to protect? I don't want anyone reading my mail. I get a post office box. I call Frosh and ask him to pass my new mailing information on to Ellen. I purposely do not give her my last name, or my phone number. Having had no control over this situation for thirty-one years, I need to measure things out, moderate the amount of contact.

The father, another name to look up in the phone book, another set of blanks to fill in. What did his name mean to the lawyer? Why did he recognize it? Who is my father?

I call a friend in Washington, a native, a man who knows things.

"Does this name ring a bell?"

There is a pause. "It does. He used to come into one of the clubs."

"Anything else?" I ask.

"That's all that comes to mind. If I think of anything I'll let you know."

"Thanks."

"Hey, is this someone you're thinking of writing about?"

The next week, without warning, my parents visit me in New York.

"Surprise, surprise."

They are being incredibly nice, warm and loving, as though I have a terminal disease—six months to live.

"We'd like to take you out to dinner," they say.

I can't go and I can't tell them why. I send them to dinner, knowing that while they are gone, I will call her.

Hers is the most frightening voice I've ever heard—low, nasal, gravelly, vaguely animal. I tell her who I am and she screams, "Oh my God. This is the most wonderful day of my life." Her voice, her emotion, comes in bursts, like punctuation—I can't tell if she is laughing or crying. In the background there is a flick, a sharp suck of air—smoking.

The phone call is thrilling, flirty as a first date, like the beginning of something. There is a rush of curiosity, the desire to know everything at once. What is your life like, how do your days begin and end? What do you do for fun? Why did you come and find me? What do you want?

Every nuance, every detail means something. I am like an amnesiac being awakened. Things I know about myself, things that exist without language, my hardware, my mental firing patterns—parts of me that are fundamentally, inexorably me are being echoed on the other end, confirmed as a DNA match. It is not an entirely comfortable sensation.

"Tell me about you—who are you?" she asks.

I tell her that I live in New York, I am a writer, I have a dog. No more or less.

She tells me that she loves New York, that her father used to come to New York and would always return with presents from FAO Schwarz. She tells me how much she loved her father, who died of a heart attack when she was seven because "he liked rich food."

This causes an immediate pain in my chest: the idea that I might die of a heart attack early in life, that I now know I need to be careful, that the things I enjoy most are dangerous.

She goes on, "I come from a very strange family. We're not quite right."

"What do you mean, strange?" I ask.

She tells me about her mother dying of a stroke a couple of years earlier. She tells me about her own life falling apart, how she moved from Washington to Atlantic City. She tells me that after she gave birth to me her mother wouldn't come to the hospital to pick her up. She had to take the bus home. She tells me that it took all her strength and courage to come looking for me.

And then she says, "Have you heard from your father? It would be nice if the three of us could get together," she says. "We could all come to New York and have dinner."

She wants everything all at once and it is too much for me. I am talking to the woman who has loomed in my mind, larger than life, for the entirety of my life, and I am terrified. There is a deep fracture in my thoughts, a refrain constantly echoing: I am not who I thought I was, and I have no idea who I am.

I am not who I thought I was, and neither is she the queen of queens that I imagined.

"I can't see you yet."

"Why can't I see you?"

I am tempted to tell her, You can't see me right now, because right now I am not visible to anyone, even myself. I have evaporated.

"When can we talk again?" she asks as we are hanging up. "When? I hope you will forgive me for what I did thirty-one years ago. When can I see you? If you said yes, I would come there right now. I would be at your door. Will you call again soon? I love you. I love you so much."

My parents return from dinner. I am looking at a picture of her, a Xerox of her driver's license that the lawyer forwarded to me. Ellen Ballman, strong, thick, fierce, like a prison matron. There is another photo in the envelope— Ellen with a niece and nephew, with stuffed animals in the background. There is something about the way feeling moves across the face—something vaguely familiar. In the cheeks, the eyes, eyebrows, forehead I see traces of myself.

"How did she have Frosh's name?" my mother wants to know.

"She said she'd heard it once and never forgot."

"Interesting," my mother says, "because Frosh wasn't the first lawyer; the first lawyer died and we got Frosh after you were born, when we were having some problems."

"What kind of problems?"

"She never signed the papers. She was supposed to sign them before she left the hospital and she didn't. And then we arranged for her to go into a bank to sign them, and she never showed up. She never signed anything and when we first went to court the judge wouldn't let us adopt you because the papers weren't signed. It took more than a year after that and then finally a second judge allowed us to adopt without a signature. For an entire year, I lived in fear. I was afraid to leave you alone with anyone except dad and Grumama, afraid if I turned around she'd come back and you'd be gone."

I think of my mother having lost a child six months before I was born, having ushered him into and out of the world. I think of her having received me as a kind of get-well gift and then worrying that at any moment I too would be gone. I don't tell my mother one of the first things Ellen Ballman said to me: "If I'd known where you were I would have come and gotten you." I don't tell my mother that it turned out that all along Ellen Ballman wasn't far away—a couple of miles. "I used to look at children," Ellen told me. "And sometimes I followed them, wondering if they were you."

*   *   *

Our conversations are frequent—I call her a couple of times a week but I don't give her my phone number. They are seductive, addictive, punishing. Each one shakes me; each requires a period of recovery. Each time I tell her something, she takes the information and holds it too close, reinventing it and delivering it back to me in a manner that leaves me wanting to tell her less, wanting her to know nothing.

She tells me that she never got along well with her step-father and that her mother was cold and cruel. I feel that there's more to the story than she's telling me. I get the sense that something was happening at home involving the stepfather, and that the mother knew and blamed her for it—which would also explain the animosity between them and why Ellen, as a teen, was propelled into the arms of a much older, married man. I never ask her the question directly. It seems intrusive; her need to protect herself is stronger than my need to know. There is an odd and anxious unknowing to much of what she says that makes it difficult to get the story straight. She reminds me of Tennessee Williams's Blanche DuBois, moving from person to person, desperate to get something, to find relief from unrelievable pain. Her lack of sophistication leaves me unsure whether she's of limited intelligence or simply shockingly naive.

"Did you think of having an abortion?"

"The thought never occurred to me. I couldn't have."

Pregnancy, I gather, was the perfect way out of her mother's house and into my father's life. It must have seemed like a good idea, until my father refused to leave his wife. He tried. He sent Ellen to Florida saying he'd join her there—and never showed up. Three months later, homesick, she returned to Washington. They got an apartment together; for four days, he lived with Ellen. Then he went back, claiming that "his children missed him." Ellen had him arrested under an old Maryland ordinance for desertion. At the time his wife was also pregnant, with a boy who was born three months before I was.

"At one point he told me to meet him at his lawyer's office," she says, "so we could figure out a way to 'take care of everything.' I sat down with him and his lawyer and the lawyer drew a diagram and said, 'There's a pie and there are only so many slices of the pie and that's all there is and it's got to go around.' 'I am not a slice of pie,' I said, and walked out. I have never been so angry in my life. Slices of pie. I told my friend Esther I was expecting a baby and didn't know what to do. She told me she knew someone who wanted to adopt a baby. I told her the baby must go to a Jewish family who would treat her well. I referred to you as 'the baby.' I didn't know if you were a boy or a girl. I couldn't take care of you myself—young ladies didn't have babies on their own."

She interrupts herself. "Do you think, one day, we might have a portrait painted of the two of us?" Her request seems to come from another world, another life. What would she do with a portrait? Hang it over her fireplace in Atlantic City? Send it to my father for Christmas? She is in stopped time, filled with fantasies of what might have been. After thirty-one years, she has returned to reclaim the life she never had.

"I have to go, I'm late for dinner," I say.

"Okay," she says. "but before you go out, put on your cashmere sweater so you don't get chilly."

I don't have a cashmere sweater.

"When can I see you?" she starts again.

"Ellen, this is all new for me. You might have thought about it for a long time before you contacted me, but for me it's only a couple of weeks. I need to take things slowly. We'll talk again soon." I hang up. The sweater is Ellen's fantasy, an image of an experience that is not my own, but one that has meaning, import elsewhere—in her past.

I am losing myself. On the street I see people who look alike—families where each face is a nuanced version of the other. I watch how they stand, how they walk and talk, variations on a theme.

A few days later, I try Ellen again.

"Ruggles slept in the hall," she says. Ruggles is the stuffed animal I sent her, in a gesture of kindness. Tonight Ruggles is me.

There is the flick of a lighter, the suck of a cigarette.

"I'm angry with you, can you tell?"

"Yes."

"Why won't you see me?" she whines. "You're torturing me. You take better care of your dog than you take of me."

Am I supposed to be taking care of her? Is that what she's come back for?

"You should adopt me—and take care of me," she says.

"I can't adopt you," I say.

"Why not?"

I don't know how to respond. I don't know if we're talking in fantasy or reality. What happened to "in the best interests of the child"? Who is the parent and who is the child? I can't say I don't want a fifty-year-old child.

"You're scaring me," is all I can manage.

"Why won't you forgive me? Why are you always angry with me?"

"I'm not angry with you," I tell her and it is entirely true. Of all the things I am, I am not angry with her.

"Don't be angry with me forever. If I'd known where you were I would have come and gotten you and taken you away." Imagine that—kidnapped by one's own mother, the same mother who had given you away at birth. She lived not two miles from where I grew up, and luckily didn't know who or where I was. I cannot imagine anything more terrifying.

"I'm not angry with you." I am horrified at the way I see myself in her—the loose screw is not entirely unfamiliar—and appalled that in the end I may end up rejecting the one person I never had any intention of rejecting. But not angry. Not unforgiving. The more Ellen and I talk, the happier I am that she gave me up. I can't imagine having grown up with her. I would not have survived.

"Have you heard from your father? I'm surprised he hasn't been in touch."

It occurs to me that "my father" may be having the same reaction to her that I'm having, that he equates me with her, and that may be one of the reasons he's keeping his distance. It also occurs to me that he may think that she and I are somehow in this together, conspiring to get something from him.

I write him a letter of my own, letting him know how surprised I was by Ellen's appearance, and suggesting that, while this is something neither he nor I asked for, we try to deal with things with some small measure of grace. I tell him a little bit about myself. I give him a way of contacting me.

I go to the gym. Overhead there is a bank of televisions, CNN, MTV, and the Cartoon Network. I am watching a cartoon in which a basket containing a baby bird is left outside a wooden door carved into the base of a tree. The words "Knock, Knock" appear on the screen. A large rooster opens the door and picks up the basket. A note is pinned to the fabric covering the basket.

Dear Lady,
Please take care of my little one.
Signed,
Big One

The rooster looks inside; a small but feisty baby bird pokes up. The rooster gets excited. An image of the baby bird in a frying pan dances in the rooster's head. A chicken wearing a bonnet comes into the house and shoos the rooster away. The rooster is disappointed. I am on the treadmill, in tears.

A couple of months pass. It is a cold night between the end of winter and the beginning of spring, and I am in Washington, D.C. I have spent an hour circling my father's house, wondering why he hasn't answered my letter.

I am a detective, a spy, a bastard. The house is large; there is a pool, a tennis court, and a lot of cars in the driveway. I sit outside under the cover of night, imagining him with his family, his wife, his other children.

I am on the outside looking in, the interior lights lay bare their lives. The lit windows are like light boxes illuminating X-rays.

From the outside, it looks as though he has it all and

then some. The walls in one of the upstairs rooms are painted a deep forest green, with white trim around the edges. I imagine it as a library.

I see a girl pull back the curtain and look out—is she my sister?

There is a For Sale sign in the front yard. I imagine calling the realtor and taking a tour, moving from room to room like a true ghost, unseen, unknown, gathering information, looking in closets, cupboards, acquiring false intimacy by passing over their things, witnessing how they live, which way they unroll the toilet paper, what books are by the side of the bed.

I sit outside the house until I have had enough and then crawl back to my parents' house.

There is a message on my answering machine at home in New York—the voice raspy, accented, coarse. "Your cover is blown. I know who you are and I know where you live. I'm reading your books."

I dial her immediately. "Ellen, what are you doing?"

"I found out who you are, A.M. Homes. I'm reading your books."

It is the only time in my life that I have regretted being a writer. She has something of mine and she thinks she has me.

"How did you get my number?"

"I'm very clever. I called all the bookstores in Washington and asked them, 'Who is a writer from Washington whose first name is Amy?' At first I thought you were someone else, some other Amy who wrote a book about God, and then one of the stores helped me and gave me your number."

She stalks me. I stop answering the phone. Every time the phone rings, every time I call in for messages, I brace myself.

"Do you live with someone on Charles Street? Is he there? Does he not like it when I call?"

"How do you know I live on Charles Street?"

"I'm a good detective."

"Ellen, I find it very upsetting. How do you know where I live?"

"I don't have to tell you," she says.

"Then I don't have to continue this conversation," I say.

"Why won't you see me? Do I have to come up there and find you? Do I have to come up to Columbia University and hunt you down? Do I have to wait in line to get your autograph?"

"I need to be able to do my job. I need to teach my classes and go on my book tour and do all the things I'm supposed to do without worrying that you are going to hunt me down. You can't do that. I have to be able to lead my life."

"I need to see you."

There are no limits. It is all about her need, incessant and total—she wants more and more. I am not allowed to have any rules. I am not allowed to say no.

Sometimes as a child, I would cry inconsolably. I would bellow, a primal cry, so deeply guttural, cellular, and thoroughly real that it would terrify my mother.

"Stop, you have to stop. Can you hear me? Please stop."

If I was able to speak at all, the only thing I would say was, "I want my mom. I want my mom." Again and again—an incantation. I would repeat it endlessly, comforting myself by rubbing back and forth over the words. "I want my mom, I want my mom."

"I'm right here," she would say. "I'm your mother. I'm all the mother you've got."

After Ellen came back, I never cried that way again. I was longing for something that never existed.

The lack of purity became clear to me—I am not my adopted mother's child, I am not Ellen's child. I am an amalgam. I will always be something glued together, something slightly broken. It is not something I might recover from but something I must accept, to live with—with compassion.

I want my mom.

"Do you wish she hadn't come back?" my mother asks. "Do you wish we hadn't told you?"

"It wasn't your secret to keep."

Do I wish she hadn't come back? Sometimes. Yes. But once it happened, I wouldn't have wanted to stop the flow of information. It is about fate, the life cycle of information. Once I know something, the amount of effort it takes to deny it, to suspend knowledge, is enormous and potentially more dangerous than to simply move along with it and see where it takes me.

Blindness—May 1993. The day my novel is published I accidentally poke the *New York Times* into my eye and shred my cornea. The pain is searing. I fumble for the eye doctor's number and go rushing off to his office, returning hours later with what looks like a maxi pad taped over my face. There is a message from my publisher letting me know that my book has been reviewed that morning in the *Washington Post*, a message from my mother saying that she's arranged for brownies and crudités to be served at my reading tomorrow in Washington, and a message from "the father."

"It's Norman," he says, his voice wobbly, tentative, choking on itself. "I got your letter. Why don't you give me a call when you have a moment."

It's been more than a month since I wrote him. If the review hadn't appeared in the *Post*, would he have called? If I'd been flipping burgers in a McDonald's instead of writing books, would I have ever heard from him?

"Well, what do you know?" he says, when I return the call. He's a swaggering big shot, but there's something to him, some half-a-heart that I instantly appreciate.

"Have you spoken to the Dragon Lady?" he asks, and I assume that he is talking about Ellen.

"She's a little crazy."

He laughs. "That's the way she always was. That's why I had to do what I did."

Norman, a former football hero, a combat veteran, for some reason feels compelled to give me a pep talk. Fifty years after the fact, he quotes what Coach once told him about staying in the game, about not being a quitter. No one has ever spoken to me this way before; there's something I like about it—it's comforting, inspiring. He couldn't be more different from the father I grew up with, an intellectual type. If I told Norman that I spent every Saturday of my childhood going to museums he wouldn't know how to respond.

"I'll be in Washington tomorrow for a couple of days on a book tour," I say.

"Why don't you meet me at my lawyer's office and we can talk."

I think of Ellen: *I am not a slice of pie.*

The next day I read in Washington; the bookstore is crowded with neighbors, relatives, my fourth-grade teacher, old friends from junior high, from early writing workshops. I haven't had a chance to tell anyone about the eye injury in advance. When I get up to read, they're shocked.

"It's fine," I say. "It'll be okay in a couple of weeks." I crack open the book. My field of vision is a circle about two inches wide. I hold the pages directly in front of my face. My good eye is half closed in sympathy with the injured one. I perform as much from memory as possible.

When the reading is finished, a long line forms, people wanting books signed, aspiring writers with questions. In the soft distance I see a stranger, a woman, standing nervously, twisting an umbrella around and around in her hands. Instinctively, I know it is Ellen. I continue signing books. The line begins to thin. Just as the last person is leaving, she steps up.

"What did you do to your eye?" she blurts in that rough voice.

"You're not behaving," I say. The store is packed with people who don't know what ghost has risen up.

"You're built just like your father," she says.

Later, when I try to remember what she looked like, I have only a vague memory of green with white polka dots, brown hair piled high on her head. I remember seeing her arm and thinking how small her bones were.

In the distance another shadow emerges. My mother and a friend of hers are coming toward me. I imagine the two mothers meeting, colliding. This is something that can't happen. It is entirely against the rules. No one person can have two mothers in the same room at the same time.

"There are people here whose privacy I have to protect," I say to Ellen. She turns and runs out of the store.

"We spotted her during the reading," my mother's friend says.

"I knew who she was immediately," my mother says. "Are you all right?" she asks—she seems shaken.

"Are *you*?"

I'm scheduled to meet with a reporter after the reading. We sit in the basement of the bookstore, the reporter's cassette recorder on a table between us.

"Is your book autobiographical?"

"It is the most autobiographical thing I have written, but no, it is not autobiographical."

"But you are adopted?"

"Yes."

"I heard something recently about you searching for your parents."

"I have not searched for anyone."

There is a pause. "Do you know who your parents are?" It seems like a strange question, like the kind of thing you'd ask someone who'd bumped their head against a wall and just regained consciousness.

*   *   *

In the morning, I take a taxi downtown. I am going to meet the father. I take a taxi because I am blind, because my mother is at work, because I can't ask my father to drive me to meet my father. I am out of time, outside of myself. It feels like something from long ago when women didn't drive. It is as though I am in a remake, a dramatic reenactment of a role originated by Ellen—the Visit to the Lawyer's Office—the scene in which the pregnant woman goes to the lawyer's office to find out what the big guy "might be able to do for her."

At the lawyer's office, I present myself to the receptionist. A man comes through the interior door. Is this the lawyer, my father, or just someone who works there? Anyone could be him, he could be anyone—this is what it's like when you don't know who you are.

I am reminded of the children's book *Are You My Mother?*—in which a baby bird goes around asking various other animals and objects, "Are you my mother?"

"Are you Norman?"

"Yes," he says, surprised that I don't already know. He shakes my hand nervously and leads me into a large conference room. We sit on opposite sides of a wide table.

"My God," he says, looking at me. "My God."

"I cut my cornea," I say, pointing to the patch on my eye.

"Reading a review of your book?"

"No, the obituaries," I say honestly.

"Fine thing. Would you like a Pepsi?" On the table in front of him is a Pepsi bottle, sweating.

I shake my head.

The father is a big, pink-faced man, in a fancy suit, collar pin, tie. His hair is white, thin, slicked back.

We stare at each other across the table. "Fine thing," he keeps saying. He is smiling. He has dimples.

Having grown up without the refracted reflections of biology, I have no idea whether he looks like me or not. I've brought my camera, a Polaroid.

"Do you mind if I take a picture of you?" I ask.

I take two and he just sits there flushed, embarrassed.

"Could I have one of you?" he asks and I allow him to take a picture.

It's as though we're making a perverse Polaroid commercial right there in the lawyer's office—a reunion played out as a photo session. We come around the table and stand side by side, watching our images appear. It's easier to really look at someone in a photograph than in real life—no discomfort at meeting the other person's eye, no fear of being caught staring. Later, when I show friends the pictures, it is obvious to everyone that he's my father— "Just look at the face, look at the hands, the ears, they're the same as yours."

Are they?

Norman hands me a copy of my book to sign. I autograph it for him and suddenly wonder what kind of a meeting we are having. I feel like a foreign diplomat exchanging official gifts.

"Tell me a little bit about you," I say.

"I'm not circumcised."

Okay, maybe it wasn't the first thing he said, but it was certainly the second. "My grandmother was a strict Catholic, she had me baptized. I'm not circumcised."

It is strange information to have about your father. We've just met and he's telling me about his dick. What he's really telling me, I guess, is that he's distanced himself from his Jewish half and that he's obsessed with his penis. He goes on to tell tales of his great-grandmother, a nineteenth-century East Prussian princess, and other relatives, who were plantation owners on the Eastern Shore of Maryland—slaveholders. He tells me I'm eligible for the Daughters of the American Revolution. He says that a family member, a British admiral, came over on either the *Arc* or the *Dove* and that there's also a connection to Helmuth von Moltke, who according to Norman said, "We will leave them with only their eyes to cry with," when leading Prussian soldiers into France in 1870. Then he goes on about our connections to the Nazis and the Death's Head Troops, as though they are something to be proud of.

"And the Dragon Lady isn't Jewish either. She likes to

think she is, but she went to Catholic school." They are both half Catholic, half Jewish. He identifies as one and she as the other.

He tells me how beautiful Ellen was when she came to work in his store. When I mention the age difference between them—she was in her mid-teens, he was thirty-two—he gets defensive, saying, "She was a slut who knew more than her years—things a young girl shouldn't know." He blames her for his lack of self-control. I ask if it ever occurred to him that something might be going on in her mother's house, something with the stepfather. He shrugs it off, and then, when pressed, says, yes, she tried to tell him something, but he didn't really know what she was talking about, and yes, maybe there was something going on at home and he probably should have tried to find out.

I ask him about their relationship: How often did he see her? Did he ever really think he might leave his wife?

He is sweating, stuffed into his good suit.

His wife knew about the affair. Ellen has told me that. Ellen has also told me that Norman sometimes brought his oldest child along when they went out. She met the younger ones too but never knew them very well.

Did Norman think he was such a big guy that he could have it all? I picture the affluence of the early sixties, highball glasses and aqua blue party dresses, Cadillac convertibles, big hair, Ellen doing a kind of demented Audrey Hepburn girl thing, Norman the swaggering football hero and veteran, the guy with a gleam in his eye, a wife at home, a young girl on the side, thinking he's got the good life.

"And what did you do for fun?" I ask, and he just looks at me. The answer is evident. Sex. The relationship was about sex, at least for him. I am the product of a sex life, not a relationship.

"She had a problem," he says. "She was a nympho-maniac. She went out with other men, lots of men."

Here I believe Ellen. How much of a nymphomaniac could a fifteen-year-old schoolgirl be? She was clever, crafty, probably trained by an expert—her mother. (I have a mental picture of Ellen's mother as Shelley Winters playing Charlotte Haze in the film version of *Lolita*.) But what Ellen looked for in Norman was comfort.

It is clear that Norman is still taken with Ellen. He asks me about her in great detail. I feel like the child of divorced parents—except that I have no idea who these people are. I have no idea what they are talking about. And what they are most interested in is talking about each other.

He tells me that he and his wife wanted to adopt me, and that Ellen wouldn't allow it. "I wanted to take care of you," he says. "After it happened, after she'd given birth, I heard that you were a boy." He looks at me as if there's something to be said.

"I'm not," I say.

"I guess it's good we didn't adopt you. My wife might have taken it out on you, she might have treated you badly."

"Yes, it's good."

"She told me she was pregnant the day my mother died."

Later, I ask Ellen about these things and she is furious. "He was never going to adopt you. He never even suggested it. I made the arrangements myself and never told him what I was going to do."

"Did you tell him you were pregnant the day his mother died?"

"Yes," she says, and there is the defiant flick of a lighter, the suck of a cigarette.

I change the subject. "Ellen told me about her father," I say to Norman. "She was very close to him and he died of a heart attack."

"He didn't die of a heart attack," Norman says, indignantly. "He was the White House bookie and he died in a shoot-out with another bookie." It makes sense. It explains a part of the story that Ellen couldn't really explain, something about men carrying her father into the house, him dying upstairs, and the family having to stay at a fancy hotel for a while.

I remember an early school field trip to Ford's Theatre—the image of Abe Lincoln being shot and then carried across the street to Petersen's Boarding House to die.

I am relieved that Ellen's father didn't have a heart attack. There are criminals in my past, but at least their hearts are strong.

"Tell me about your people," Norman says. He asks about "my people" as though I was raised by wolves. Clearly, my people are not the same as "his people."

"My people," I tell him, "are lovely. You couldn't ask for better." I owe him nothing. My people are Jews, Marxists, socialists, homosexuals. There is nothing about me, about my life, that he would understand.

We are winding down. I am exhausted.

"I'd like to take you into my family, to introduce you to your brothers and sister. You have three brothers and a sister. But before I can do that, my wife wants everything to be clear. She wants a test to prove that you are my child.

"Would you consider a blood test? You wouldn't have to pay for it." It's the "You wouldn't have to pay for it" that throws me. Is this what I get as my big reward, the reparation for the wrongs of the past—a DNA test? And what's behind Door Number Three? Insulting as this is, on some level I can't blame him. Throwing it to science might be a good idea—it might make fact out of what feels like fiction.

"I'll think about it," I say.

"Fine thing."

In the middle of July 1993, I agree to the DNA test. Norman and I make a plan to meet at a lab. I take the train to D.C.

It is less a lab and more a collection center, a bureaucratic black hole, the most generic office ever made. The fluorescent lighting works like an X-ray throwing everything into relief.

Norman is there waiting—the only white man in the room. It's the first time I've seen him since the lawyer's office. We sit next to each other, the metal chairs are linked together—forced closeness.

We wait.

They call Norman's name. He tries to give them a personal check, but they won't take it. There are signs everywhere detailing how payment is to be made: all checks must be certified. He offers to get them the cash, but they can't accept cash, only certified checks. He goes to the bank downstairs and for some reason is unable to get one. He returns, flustered, humiliated. He insists that the technician make a call, that he try to get an exception, but it is all to no avail. The check and the blood must be sent together. Because this test is often part of a lawsuit, the lab insists on being paid in advance to avoid the complication of collection. This is the stuff of murders, rapes, proof. Are you or are you not my father?

The next morning we try again.

"Long time no see," I say.

"What if we get in there and the nurse is the Dragon Lady? She'll come at us with a square, blunt-tipped needle," Norman jokes nervously. I laugh but it is not funny. We have a tacit agreement not to tell Ellen what we are doing. What we are doing is insulting to her.

The technician calls in a small child who is ahead of us. The little boy screams when they take him.

"You're not going to do that, are you?" Norman asks.

Worse, I'm thinking, far, far worse.

As Norman walks up to the counter, I notice that his butt looks familiar; I am watching him and I'm thinking: There goes my ass. That's my ass walking away. His blue sport coat covers it halfway, but I can see it broken into sections, departments of ass, high and low just like mine. I notice his thighs—chubby, thick, not a pretty thing. This is the first time I have seen anyone else in my body.

I stare as he turns and comes back to me. I look down at his shoes, white loafers, country-club shoes, stretched out, fading. Inside the shoe, his feet are wide and short. I look up; his hands are the same as mine, square like paws. He is an exact replica, the male version of me.

"Fine thing," Norman says, seeing me stare.

I go first. I roll up my sleeve. The technician pulls on his gloves, assembles his tubes, and ties the rubber tourniquet around my arm. I make a fist. Norman is watching.

The needle goes in, a sharp metal prick.

I look at Norman. It feels strange. I am giving blood for this man, I am letting my flesh be punctured to prove that I am of him. It is beyond sexual.

"Let go of the fist," the technician says and I relax my hand.

The blood is drawn, tubes and tubes of it, and then there is cotton on my wound and a Band-Aid over it.

I have allowed this because I understand the need for proof, for some true measure of our relationship, and also because I have a fantasy that there is something in it for me, that Norman will keep his word, that he will take me into his family, that I will suddenly have three brothers and a sister—a new and improved spare family.

"Please sign here." The technician hands me the tubes, one at a time.

"What?"

"You have to sign the tubes."

They are warm in my palm, filled with the chemical sum of who and what I am. I sign quickly, hoping not to faint. I am holding myself in my hands.

Norman is next. He takes off his jacket, revealing short shirt sleeves, sad-old-guy style. His arms are plump, pale, almost fluffy. There is something so white about him, so

soft, so exposed that it is perverse. He lays out his arm.
The technician ties it off, swabs it, and I look away unable
to watch this strange genetic striptease.

I am sickened by it all. I wait in the hall. I do not watch
him holding his blood, signing his tubes. He comes out of
the room, puts his jacket back on, and we are out the door.

"I would have liked to take you for a nice lunch if
you'd worn something better," he says when we are in the
hallway.

I am dressed perfectly well—in linen pants and a
blouse. DNA testing is not a black-tie occasion. I am
tempted to say, That's okay—I would have liked you to be
my father if you weren't such a jerk. But I am so stunned
that I become stupidly apologetic. I am not wearing what
he wanted; I am not wearing a dress. I am not meeting his
fantasy of his daughter.

We go to a less-than-mediocre restaurant down the
block. People seem to know him there. He introduces me
to the maître d' as though that means something. We sit
down. The tablecloths are green, the napkins polyester.

"You don't wear jewelry," Norman says.

I am single, I live in New York City, I am not wearing a
dress. I know exactly what he is thinking.

I say nothing. Later, I'll wish that I'd said something,
I'll wish that I'd told him the truth. I have no jewelry, but
if you want to throw me some diamonds I'd be glad to
wear them. I come from a family that doesn't do that sort

of thing. I grew up boycotting grapes and iceberg lettuce because they weren't picked by union workers.

What kind of father makes his child travel to another city to prove that she is his child and then criticizes her for not wearing the right clothes to the blood test, for not wearing jewelry she doesn't own to the lunch she didn't know she was having?

"How will you feel if the test comes back and I'm not your father?"

You're my father, I think. I wasn't positive before, but now, seeing you, seeing your ass, my ass—I'm sure.

The heat is stupefying. I am being twisted like pulled taffy. I walk as though I have been hit with something, blasted. I have become a stranger to myself.

To be adopted is to be adapted, to be amputated and sewn back together again. Whether or not you regain full function, there will always be scar tissue.

Back at the house, my mother wants to do something to make it better. She takes me on a picnic. We go to Candy Cane City—the park of my childhood—and sit at a table under the trees looking out at the merry-go-round, the swing set, the aluminum slide. All of it empty now, deserted in this scorching heat wave. I put my hand on the slide, the metal is searingly hot—it feels good.

My mother unwraps a bologna sandwich. This is proof of how hard she is trying. In our house there is no bologna, no white bread. This is my favorite sandwich from childhood, the one I got only for field trips and special occasions. She pulls a bag of potato chips and a cold Coke out of the bag, replicating my earliest idea of the sublime. We look out at the tennis courts, the basketball hoops, the water fountain, all of it indelibly etched in my memory. I could come to this park in my sleep, just as I have come to it often in my fiction.

"Take me for a ride," I say.

"Tomorrow," she says. "Tomorrow I'll take the day off work and we'll go somewhere."

In the morning we leave. The motion of the car is soothing—it makes up for my inability to move myself, it fulfills my need for someone else to move me, to carry me. The road unfolds.

I don't tell my mother what happened when I went for the blood test, I do not tell her how truly depressed I am. I don't say anything because anything I say will make her anxious, angry, and then I will have to deal with her feelings. And at the moment I am struggling to understand my own.

I wish I had a video of Norman, of his ass walking away. I wish I had him on tape saying, You're not dressed right. I wish I had Ellen on audio, her misplaced projections, her odd habit of seeming to confuse me with her dead mother, accusing me of not paying enough attention to her, not doing enough for her.

I wish I had it all in such a way that it could be labeled and laid out on a long table—as evidence.

My mother is driving us into the past, to Berkeley Springs, West Virginia, a dark, dank old town. This is where George Washington went when he wanted to take a soak; home of the oldest mineral bath in the country—my grandparents used to take us here.

This is a place from my past that feels familiar, untouchable, unchanged. I am glad to be returned to something that predates me. The bathhouse is divided into ladies' and men's; everyone there is a million years old, dating directly back to George Washington. I imagine it is like a Swedish sanitarium; there is something deeply medicinal about it—we have come for a cure.

Soaking in the holy antique waters is cleansing— lying on the slab of a table while an old woman kneads my flesh is equal to the moment I am in. It is the perfect escape.

We have our treatments and then we go to the old hotel for club sandwiches and head home.

On the phone, Norman tells me he has something for me, something he wants to give me; first he tells me he will send it to me and then he says he will wait and give it to me in person. I am thinking it is a family heirloom, something of his, of his mother's, something that came on the *Arc* or the *Dove*, something that the Nazi brought back, something that his father gave his mother, something that he wanted to give Ellen. Whatever it is, he never gives it to me, he never mentions it again.

Over the next few months, we meet several more times. We meet in hotels. We meet at Holiday Inns, Marriotts, Comfort Inns, Renaissance Quarters, in the odd spaces that are between spaces, the there that is never there.

We meet in the lobby, awkwardly kiss hello, and then move to the glass atrium, or the inner courtyard, or the café, looking up at a surround of numbered doors, house-keeping carts making their rounds. We come from the outside and are plunged into a temperature-controlled en-vironment where the potted plants are watered automati-cally, where they are rotated seasonally like crops, where everything is suspended in time—hermetically sealed.

Ever since Norman's comment about my clothing, I worry about what I am wearing, how I look. I continually feel that I am being evaluated. I want his approval. There is something about him that I like—the bigness of him; he is grandiose, larger than life. Sometimes it scares me; sometimes it lures me into another world, a world of men.

There is something sleazy about it, meeting in the middle of the afternoon in these middle-of-the-road ho-tels. Does he think that these are safe places where no one will see us? Does he have something in mind? It is never clear to me why we are meeting in them.

"You don't know what it does to me to look at you," he says.

He doesn't mean, The resemblance is amazing, or, I'm so proud of what you've done with your life.

"You don't know what it does to me to look at you." He says it in a strange way. He is looking at me and seeing someone else.

He never does anything to push it further but I am always thinking that he will. I imagine him saying, I've got a room, I want to see you naked. I imagine undressing as part of the procedure of proving who I am, part of the degradation.

I imagine him fucking me.

I imagine being Ellen and him fucking her thirty-one years ago.

I imagine something profoundly sad.

It is the strangest set of imaginings and I can tell he has them too.

I have read about this; it is not unusual for the primal experiences of parent and child to morph—the intensity, the intimacy of the sensations is often expressed in adults as sexual attraction. But while the attraction may be common, almost expected, obviously it cannot be explored.

He makes no mention of the blood test—the results can take eight to twelve weeks. He makes no mention of telling his other children about me. Instead he tells me about how fond he is of his grandchildren. He tells me how close he was to his grandmother. And again he tells me how Coach always used to tell him to stay in the game—never get out of the game.

He asks me if I've spoken with her.

"Yes," I say. "Have you?"

He nods, yes.

"She wants to visit me," I tell him. "She sends letters with fantasies about going to the Central Park Zoo, for walks by the ocean, out to dinner. She has no idea of how strange this is for me. And she's unrelenting—she could take over my life, she could swallow me whole."

He smiles. "She's a stubborn lady."

"She wants to know when the three of us can have dinner together."

He says nothing.

"Maybe you two should have dinner sometime?"

Norman blushes. "I don't think so." He shakes his head as if to say, You know what would happen. If he so much as saw her again, they would be back at it. He is still afraid of the power she has over him. I have the sense that he has promised himself or, more, that he has promised his wife that he won't see her. A lot more has happened than I'll ever know.

He shifts in his chair. He is always uncomfortable.

"Old injuries," he says, "from the war, from football. I can't sit still for very long."

There is a pause.

"My wife is jealous of you," he says.

On the rare occasions when I call Norman and his wife answers the phone, she never acknowledges who I am, never asks how I am, never says anything beyond, "Hold the line," and then goes off in search of him.

There are times when I'm tempted to say something, something simple, like, "And how are you?" or, "I'm sorry for all the trouble," but then I remember that it is not my responsibility. I can't do all the work.

"Hold the line."

Ellen thinks I'm her mother, Norman thinks I am Ellen, and I feel like Norman's wife thinks I am the mistress reincarnate.

In September of 1993, I am in a suburban Maryland emergency room with my grandmother, who has fallen and broken her hip. I'm checking messages while waiting for the radiologist to read her X-rays. Norman has left a message.

By the time I get back to my parents' house, it's late. I return the call. Norman answers the phone.

"How are you?" he asks.

I tell him about my grandmother.

"I have some information for you," he says.

I say nothing. I am not in the mood for games.

"The test results," he says.

"Do you want to tell me something?" I ask.

"Should we meet at the hotel?"

"Which hotel?"

"The one in Rockville."

"Sure," I say. "But why don't you just tell me what the results are?"

"Everything is fine," he says.

"What does that mean?"

"Everything is fine. We'll talk when I see you. Tomorrow at four?"

Everything is not fine. My patience is running thin. All of this is a game, a game that Ellen and Norman are playing, and I'm the object in the middle, the thing tossed back and forth. He's making it worse, throwing in a night of suspense, leaving me to stay up late, wondering. More than wondering if he is or isn't my father, I wonder why I keep going back for more. I will never know the whole story. There is an enormous amount that no one is telling me.

I meet him at the hotel. We are in the fern bar, the glassy atrium—the scene is like something from a science-fiction movie, a futuristic bioenvironment, the lunchroom in a space lab.

"I have the results of the DNA test," he says.

"Yes."

The waitress arrives and takes our order. I want nothing.

"I'm fine," I tell her.

"Not even some tea?" Norman asks.

"Not even tea," I say.

"Water?" the waitress asks.

"No."

Norman waits until his ginger ale arrives before he says anything.

"The test says it's ninety-nine-point-nine percent likely that I'm your father." There is a pause. "So what are my responsibilities?"

I am not a slice of pie.

"So what are my responsibilities?"

I say nothing.

Norman doesn't mention his children, or how he is going to take me into his family, or give me the large gift behind Door Number Three. He sips his drink and stares at me.

"Now that I'm your father, I think I have the right to ask—are you dating anyone?"

"No." I am unsure whether I am answering the question or refusing to answer.

"Have you told your children?" I ask.

"No, not yet," he says.

I'm wondering if he meets his other children for tea in cheap hotels.

We leave without saying good-bye, without a plan for what happens next.

*   *   *

In October I am in Washington to give a reading. Norman finds out and leaves a message. "Fine thing," he says. "You're in town? Would you like to meet?"

I call him back. "Hold the line," his wife says.

"Imagine that," Norman says, picking up. "You and my daughter in the same newspaper on the same day."

I have no idea what he's talking about.

"In the *Gazette* there are pictures of you and my daughter. Isn't that something?" He sounds oddly proud, two of his children in the pages of the local paper.

"You and my daughter . . ."

I am the ghost, the one who does not exist. When I look in the mirror, do I see my reflection?

"Have you figured out how to tell them?" I ask.

"No," he says. "I'm still having a little bit of trouble with that." He makes it sound like something he's trying to fix himself, a car part that requires tinkering. I have the feeling that his wife is stopping him.

He changes the subject, dividing his families. He asks if I've spoken with Ellen.

"She's threatening to move to New York."

"Yep. She said something to me about it—she's been up there a lot lately. I think she was going back for an interview just the other day."

Hair rises on the back of my neck—I am suddenly cold. Ellen has not mentioned that she's actually been in the city. The fact that she's been coming into town and not telling me is more frightening than if I knew. Has she been hanging around outside my building watching me? Has she been tracking me from a distance?

If Ellen moves to New York I will leave. I cannot be in the same place as her.

"Would you like to meet at the hotel?"

"No. I'm going back first thing in the morning."

Norman chuckles. "I just can't get over it," he says. "You and your sister in the same paper, what do you make of that?"

I am thinking of Ellen moving to New York. I am thinking of his other daughter, in the same newspaper. Washington is not safe anymore. New York is not safe. No place is home. I get in my mother's car and drive. It is pouring rain. I drive, hurling myself through space, as though I am driving toward something, as though it is an emergency. I want to see the sister, I want to know what he is so proud of. It is rush hour, the streets are filled with water. On the radio the newscaster is saying, "We're in the middle of a torrential downpour. There are power outages, flash flood warnings."

The paper is local, deeply local. You can only get it in a small radius around where Norman lives—which is near where I will be reading. It is like a scene from a movie. I am obsessed, there is no stopping me. I drive past broken-down cars—police are directing traffic with flares. Oblivious. I am going to meet my sister—well, not meet her, but at least see her.

When I get to the shopping center near Norman's house, I park the car and hurry into a little card store. I pick up a stack of copies of the paper and run back to the car.

The papers are wet, the newsprint sticks together, it shreds as I pull at it, the rain stains the pages, the sides bleed and blur. I find the picture of myself—it is the publicity photo from the book, strangely formal and out of place with what is happening now. I am there looking out, oblivious to what is happening now. I scan the page. "Dress Like a Doll." The article is about a Barbie children's fashion show at McDonald's. There is a photograph of Norman's granddaughter dressed like a Barbie. Norman's daughter, my sister, is almost invisible. She is sitting on a chair, bending over, wearing a large hat that blocks most of her face. She is wearing white pants with some sort of polka-dotted thing around her waist, a scarf belt. Is she dressed right for a nice lunch? Does she own jewelry?

I look at the picture carefully—I see her fat thigh, her belly, her feet, her outstretched hand, and it is my thigh, my belly, my feet, my hand.

There is something deeply ironic and pathetic about the whole thing. I am staring at a piece of wet newsprint trying to see what my sister, who doesn't even know she has a sister, looks like. There is an incredible sense of disappointment. She is in a McDonald's with her kid dressed up like a Barbie doll, and all I can think of is the short story I wrote, *A Real Doll*, about a boy dating a Barbie doll. I was being ironic; she is being serious. And to top it off—Norman thinks this picture of his daughter taking her kids to a fashion show at McDonald's is equal to an article on me giving a reading from my third book. His daughter went to finishing school, had a debutante coming-out ball, and now does "interiors." She has fat thighs, a belly, and paws for hands, but I'm sure she dresses right for lunch. It's depressing as hell.

Drenched, I return to my parents' house. I have ten minutes to get ready for the reading.

I go alone. Ever since the night Ellen appeared without warning at the bookstore, I am afraid of what might happen. My parents want to come, but I excuse them. I am protecting them as well as myself. The library where I'm reading is en route to Norman's house and just down the road from Uncle George. I have no idea if Ellen has told her brother about me or if they are even speaking. I never know who knows what.

Libraries are sacred, preserved spaces where people are supposed to behave well; they are trusted places for people who love books.

I am oddly ill at ease. From the moment I arrive, I have

the sense they are there—exactly who, I'm not sure—but I can tell I am being watched, sized up. There is the strange sensation that something else is going on—there are people here who have come for a reason other than to hear me read. No one approaches me, no one identifies themselves or makes themselves known in any way. It is incredibly eerie.

The librarian introduces me and I stand to read. The lights onstage are bright; I cannot see far enough into the audience to memorize every face. I wish I had guards on either side of the stage, looking out on my behalf, reading the crowd, identifying faces, reporting into their lapel pins.

I read from a work in progress. The crowd follows closely. There are book club ladies, friends from high school, fans with first editions, people who are habitués of that library, but there is something else, some unnameable force field. I am on display, I feel myself being watched, scanned, and yet I am obligated to keep reading, to pretend I don't know this is happening. Do they think I don't know they're out there, that I'm oblivious to them, that they are invisible, anonymous, in the dark?

I wish I could turn the lights around, shine them into the audience, I have some questions of my own. I am tempted to pull a Lenny Bruce, stop the show, and address the mystery guests, imploring them to reveal themselves— hey, you spies from the other planet, it's October, the least you could do is put on a Halloween costume, maybe show up looking like a skeleton or something. But it would look as if I'd lost my mind.

At the end of the reading, the librarian asks if I am willing to answer questions from the audience. "I'd be happy to." Hands go up.

I used to believe that every question deserved an answer, I used to feel obligated to answer everything as fully and honestly as possible. I don't anymore.

"Where do your ideas come from?" someone asks.

"From you," I say. The crowd laughs. I look at the woman asking the question; she seems innocent enough. I continue. "I get them from looking at the world we live in, from reading the paper, watching the news. It seems as though what I write is often extreme, but in truth it happens every day."

There are questions posed as challenges, tests. I have the sense that depending on my answer, they might say, You're lying, I know this and that fact about you.

I point to a raised hand.

"Do you write autobiographically?"

I feel the watchers zooming in.

"No." I say. "I have yet to write anything that is truly autobiographical."

They are taunting me.

"Are you adopted?"

"Yes, and I'm coming up for adoption again soon, so if

anyone is interested, please let the librarian at the back of the room know." More laughter.

"Do you know who your parents are? Have you searched?"

"I am always searching," I say, "but no, I have not searched in that way."

December 18, 1993. My birthday, the lightning rod, the axis around which I spin. I hold myself braced against it— an anticelebration.

How can a person with no history have a birthday? Are you sure it's my birthday? Are you sure of how old I am? How do you know? What proof do you have?

I was born in 1961. My birth certificate was issued in 1963. Is that normal? Was there a delay because I belonged to no one, hovered in limbo land, waiting to become someone?

For those two missing years did I have another name?

To add to the confusion, my birthday is in the middle of the holiday season; it features not only all the standard natal elements, but also the ongoing and age-old battle of the Christians versus the Jews, which oddly turns out to be among the battles of my biological origins.

December, the season of joy, is the season of my secret sorrows.

Every year I cannot help but think of the woman who gave me away. I find myself missing someone I never knew, wondering, Does she miss me? Does she shop for the things I buy myself? Does my father know I exist? Do I have siblings? Does anybody know who I am? I spend weeks grieving.

At this point it would take nothing short of a national monthlong festival, a public parade celebrating my existence, to reassure me that my presence on this planet is welcome. And even then I'm not sure I would believe it, I'm not sure I wouldn't doubt that it was an attempt to humor me, to temporarily cajole me out of a black hole.

And this year is something entirely new, more awful, like going back to scratch and starting all over again, a new birthday with an old child, the first with four parents instead of two, a schizoid dividing of the zygote further than the gods intended it to go.

Everyone is at me, wanting something.

My parents, who usually do nothing, are trying to plan a trip to New York. I quickly put them off.

And Ellen is calling me every night begging that she be allowed to see me, feeling that in some way this is her birthday too.

"It's your birthday," she says. "Please, pretty please." And she starts to cry, and then there is the click of the lighter and "Can you hold on for a minute while I get a drink of water?"

She writes a letter saying that Decembers have plagued

her for the last thirty-one years, she finds them excruciating, depressing, and so forth. And while it's nice to know I was never forgotten, it's stranger still that I am never known.

Norman calls asking if I've "got any big plans." He says he is sending something; he has spoken with Ellen about what would be a good gift and he's putting it in the mail—insured, overnight express, to be sure it gets there in time.

I spend the official day in hiding. I turn off the phone, I don't answer the buzzer.

Later I go downstairs and find that people have left me flowers and gifts, similar to the way strangers leave offerings at scenes of tragic accidents. My friends have created a veritable altar to the birthday girl: an FTD Pick Me Up bouquet, a get-well card, and so on.

Norman sent a small heart-shaped gold locket, the kind that snaps open and you put two pictures in, the kind that you'd give a little girl. It is such a strange gift for a thirty-two-year-old. Is this jewelry? It is more like pre-jewelry, like a training bra. (For Christmas he will send me a thin cashmere sweater—which will make me wonder, is this the kind of "cashmere sweater" Ellen was referring to?)

Ellen sends a birthday card meant for a small child—shaped like a teddy bear, signed, "Love, Mommy Ellen."

She sends a kiddie card, a silky nightgown negligee like something Mrs. Robinson would wear, and a box of homemade candy from her favorite Atlantic City candy store. The chocolate is thick, heavy, rolled, filled—it looks like it could bend your mind. I can't keep the things she sends me and I can't throw them out either. I give the chocolate away. That evening I make each of my friends take a piece, like communion wafers, bits of the mother. "Here," I say pushing the box forward, refusing to try one myself. "Take one," and I watch to see how it goes down.

Christmas Eve—it's a year since this started unfolding. I'm on the train to Washington—it's packed, the mood is festive, the luggage racks are bursting with ornately wrapped packages. I'm bringing presents even though my mother has told me we don't celebrate Christmas. The fact is we don't celebrate Hanukkah either.

We handle the holidays by pretending they aren't happening, by ignoring them. We hold our breath—it'll pass. An invisible cloud hangs over the house, a depressed charcoal gray, like the set for a Eugene O'Neill play.

Some part of me thinks it's not hard to have a decent holiday; you choose what holiday you like and you celebrate. Every year I become all the more determined that I will do it for myself, I will make my own holiday.

The winter I turned nine, I was fixated on having a

Christmas tree. It made no sense to me that all up and down the block every house except ours had a tree.

"We're Jewish," my mother said. "Jews don't have trees."

"We weren't always Jewish, were we?" Until then we'd always celebrated Christmas, a treeless Christmas, but Christmas nonetheless. I remembered leaving a plate of cookies for Santa, waking to find it empty, replaced by a long red stocking hanging from the fireplace, an orange bulging in the toe, walnuts spilling out the top, presents on the hearth. It wasn't my imagination. Until then we'd been like everyone else, and then suddenly we were different.

"I was wrong," my mother said. "It was my error. Jews don't celebrate Christmas, we have Hanukkah, the Festival of Lights."

"But the Solomons next door are Jewish too, and they have a tree."

"That's their problem," she said.

It wasn't as though we were especially religious. On Yom Kippur, the highest of the holy days, the Day of Atonement, a day of fasting, we paused only momentarily for God to count us in and then ate a late breakfast. But now, without warning, Christmas had changed its name to Hanukkah. It came early and lasted for eight days, like a plague.

We gathered around a menorah and lit the candles—
no one knew the prayer; instead we said thanks. And
thanks a lot. And is it returnable?

After the fourth night my brother refused to participate. "I've had more than enough," he said, refusing to
leave his room.

From my bedroom window I could see the neighbors'
tree twinkling with glass icicles, miniature white lights,
colored balls, tinsel.

On the day after Christmas, my mother took me to the
library. Next to the library was a Christmas tree lot. I
sneaked over and talked to the guy. It took a surprising effort to convince him—on the day after Christmas—to take
pity on a nine-year-old who lived in a house without a
tree, but he finally gave me a puny Christmas tree. I
dragged it to the car, stuffed it in the backseat, met my
mother back in the library. I was bursting with excitement
at my ingenious sneakery, beside myself with joy. Back at
the house, I slipped out and was dragging the tree from
the car, into the house, when my mother started yelling,
"What are you doing? You can't bring that in here, it's a
tree."

"Why not, why not? It's just a tree."

"Not in the living room, you're not going to put that
in the living room."

"Why can't we be like everyone else?"

"Because we're Jewish," my mother said.

And so the tree went in my room. I knew nothing about trees, about tree stands; I put it in a Maxwell House coffee can. The tree listed to one side. I propped it against the wall. It was a pathetic tree, scrawny, a tree no one wanted. But it was my tree, my Charlie Brown tree. I loved my tree, I watered it, decorated it with construction-paper loop chains and popcorn on a thread. Despite my good care, the tree died; it went from green to brown and brittle. As I dragged the tree out of the house, the needles, once soft and supple, now sharp like thorns, fell everywhere. I dragged the tree out of the house, across the yard, down around back, and hurled it down the hill. Back inside, my mother already had the Electrolux out and was working the long wand, the power brush, up and down the hall.

And now, again, it is Christmas. Waking up in the twin bed of my childhood, I do not jump up and hurry into the living room to see what Santa has brought me. I lie there thinking, it is only one day, there is no reason that today has to be so awful, so different from any other day. I take a breath and tell myself I will make it good.

The telephone rings. I hear my mother in the kitchen, answering it. She calls my name.

"How are you? I just wanted to wish you a wonderful Christmas. What are you up to today?" Norman asks.

"Nothing," I say.

I don't think he believes me.

"I'm just getting ready to go to church with the family. Just on my way out but I wanted to say hello. Ho ho ho."

There is a pause.

"Have you heard from the Dragon Lady?"

"She's with friends in Atlantic City; they're going to a show at one of the casinos, Wayne Newton or something."

"Fine thing," he says.

"Isn't it?" I say.

"Listen, I don't know how long you're in town . . . I'm not going to be able to get together today, but maybe later in the week, if you're still around, we can meet."

"I'm not sure," I say, thinking that at any minute I'll spontaneously combust and leave a smoldering heap of ashes on the floor for my mother to suck up with her Electrolux wand.

"Well, listen, you have a nice day and we'll talk soon."

"Yeah, you too. Merry Christmas." I hang up. Norman the good Christian is off to church, leaving his "other" daughter trapped like some Cinderella in the house without holidays.

I go into the kitchen. "Are you all right?" my mother asks.

"Fine," I say, slamming the refrigerator. "I'm perfectly fine."

"Do you want a bagel?"

I am picturing roasted turkeys, hams, a large luxurious dinner—too much pie.

"What does ham taste like?"

"It's good," my mother says.

"Why don't we ever have ham?"

"Your father doesn't really like meat—he thinks he's a vegetarian."

Despite my thinking I will make it a decent day, I cave in. Norman is going to church with his family and then having Christmas dinner, and they have a fucking Christmas tree. I know because late last night I drove by the house, and I saw the driveway filled with cars, a wreath on the door, a thousand lights inside.

In the afternoon, my mother does the winter equivalent of spring cleaning—she is on a stepladder in the closet. "Does any of this mean anything to you?" She shows me an old frying pan, a cookie tin, a chipped plate.

"No."

"I'm thinking of going to a movie," I say.

"Do you think you'll get in?" my mother asks.

My father is in the living room reading. "What are you thinking of seeing?

"*Schindler's List.*"

"I read a review that was negative," my father says.

"Bye. Have fun," my mother says.

"It's not supposed to be fun. That's why I'm going."

*   *   *

I grew up convinced that every family was better than mine. I grew up watching other families in awe, hardly able to bear the sensations, the nearly pornographic pleasure of witnessing such small intimacies. I would hover on the edge, knowing that however much they include you—invite you to dinner, take you on family trips—you are never official, you are always the "friend," the first one left behind.

The movie theater is crowded with families, with couples, young and old. I find a single seat in the middle of a row—everyone rises to let me pass. I'm sitting in the theater by myself, distinctly aware that I do not want to spend the rest of my life alone, frightened that I will never be able to make a life, that I am too fractured to connect with another person.

The film, taken from a novel by Thomas Keneally, is based on the true story of Oskar Schindler, a German businessman, a Nazi, a womanizer, who ultimately turned around and saved the lives of eleven hundred Jews. I watch thinking of Norman, Norman as Schindler—German, Catholic, charismatic, charming, struggling with right versus wrong. I watch prison camp commandant Goeth, who shoots Jews for target practice, thinking of the randomness, the unpredictability, of history. Even those who seem decent or even perhaps heroic aren't; instead they are human, deeply flawed. It is about the degradation of the soul, struggling to maintain some small sense of self amid so much loss, struggling to maintain oneself in a death camp, to remain human, alive, even in death. It is the Christians versus the Jews, the dividing of families, oddly relevant.

If Norman were truly the big guy, the good Christian he pretends to be, he would accept responsibility. He would tell his children that there had been a lapse in the marriage, but that something good had come of it—me.

On all sides of me people are weeping, and yet I am finding the film uplifting—it is equal to what I am feeling.

I drive home. The lights are on; I am in front of the house, the only house we ever lived in, in front of my family. I pull into the carport. I am so angry, so sad, hating everyone for who they are and for everything they are not. It is the rising of emotion, as everything I can't articulate begins whirling inside me. I gun the engine. I imagine driving the car into the house, crashing through, desperate to get past what is blocking me. I am gunning the engine, wishing I'd take my foot off the brake; the car is straining under my foot. The car, a brainless machine, wants to go forward, to hurl itself blindly through the wall and into the kitchen. I picture the cabinets emptying out, dishes breaking, the engine punching through the back of the refrigerator, a headlight coming through the crisper door. I hope the dog isn't in the kitchen, that no one has gone in for a snack. I sit with my foot on the gas, wanting to do it, and then thinking about my mother and my mother's dishes, how much she loves her dishes, how much I love my mother, how I wouldn't want to break the dishes and how it wouldn't be quite the same if I went into the house first and emptied all the shelves and then came back out again and went crashing through.

I pull up outside the house and I don't want to go home. There is no home, there is no relief, no sense of having simply survived.

Christmas is almost over. I do not want this to be the most depressing story ever told. I turn off the engine. I wait.

In January 1994, just after the new year, Ellen calls and asks, "When will you see me?"

I say, "Saturday."

She is shocked. So am I. I'm not sure why I say Saturday; but in some way it feels inevitable. How much longer can it go on: *When will you see me? Why won't you see me?* We need to meet in an agreed-upon way—and not in a kamikaze attack like the scene in the bookstore. There is no good time, no right time. I am repelled and I am also curious.

I say Saturday and immediately regret it.

She gets too excited. "Where will we meet? What will we do?" Ellen envisions the meeting as a fun-filled-day-in-New-York package—horse-drawn carriages, ice cream sodas, going to a show (by this she means a musical).

I'm thinking an hour, maybe two. I'm thinking a little bit will go a long way.

"Let's meet at the Plaza," she says. "At the Oyster Bar."

The Plaza is a part of the fantasy—home of Eloise, four o'clock tea, a tourist attraction. The last time I was there, Zsa Zsa Gabor was in the lobby talking the man at the candy store into giving her free chocolates.

"Will you let her kiss you hello?" a friend asks.

"I don't think so," I say and then feel bad. "If she wants to kiss my hand, she can."

All of the books on adoption and reunion say to arrange for someone to meet you after the reunion for a kind of deprogramming session, to pick up the pieces. I call a friend, a woman with children and grandchildren of her own, and arrange for her to meet me in the Oak Bar at 6 P.M. I tell her that if I'm not there, she's supposed to come into the Oyster Bar and get me. This is in case the mother tries to somehow detain me, to put me under her spell, in case I lose my free will and have to be plucked from my mother's clutches.

"Can I meet your mother?" the friend asks.

"Sure, I guess," I say. It seems odd that the friend is more excited, more interested in meeting my mother than

I am. It seems strange, but at the moment everything seems strange.

"No," she says. "I guess that wouldn't be right. You'll tell me about her. And maybe take a picture."

I would like to go as myself, not my best self or average self, but my worst self. In the end, I dress up. I am once again compelled to try to make a good impression. In some fantasy of my own, I want her to see how well I turned out, want her to be proud of me.

In the hallway outside the Oyster Bar she is wearing a fluffy white fur jacket, a printed silk blouse, and slacks, her hair piled high on her head in a post-beehive bun. She looks like someone from another decade—a woman who believes in glamour, who listens to Burt Bacharach and Dinah Shore to cheer herself up. I suspect this is the way she must have dressed when she used to meet my father—probably also in hotels—but now she's fifty-five years old and a lot has been lost to time.

"Is that you?" she asks, breathless.

"I can't believe it," she says, her voice escalating beyond giddy and into a husky sort of mania—on the verge. "I can't believe I'm seeing you."

She takes my hand and kisses it.

Before anything else happens I want to run to a pay phone and call my friend. "Remember when you asked me if I was going to kiss her . . . well, she kissed my hand.

Did she know we had that conversation? Is my phone tapped? Is this the difference between what one is born as and what one becomes, hardware versus software, nature versus nurture?"

She kisses my hand and I want to run.

I follow her into the restaurant. She orders a Harveys Bristol Cream, I order a Coke. I have never seen someone drink Harveys Bristol Cream. I only remember it from ads; suave couples in front of a fireplace, drinking Harveys.

I feel suddenly defensive; under her gaze, I sense I am not measuring up. She is sitting there in her old rabbit jacket and I am across from her in my best clothes. She never graduated high school and I have multiple master's degrees. She is the one who for months begged to meet me and I am the one who avoided her. I tell myself it is not about surfaces. I tell myself everything will be all right.

"I'm having lobster," she says.

"And what will you have?" the waiter asks.

"Nothing, I will have nothing." I have nothing, I am nothing. Nothing suits me fine.

"Have lobster," she says.

I am allergic to lobster. "Nothing is good," I tell the waiter.

She talks about Atlantic City. She says that she has left her job—I don't know if that means quit or was fired—and is going to open a beauty parlor with a couple of "wonderful operators." She talks, about anything, everything, without the awareness that the person sitting across from her is both her only child and a complete stranger.

Her lobster arrives, she pulls meat from the claw, dips it into a silver pot of butter, and pops it into her mouth. She brings the claw to her eye, looking to see if there is more. Nothing is enough. I stare, wondering how she can eat. I can barely breathe.

"Did your father send you something for your birthday? He was going to send you something very nice."

I can't help but remember the gold-plated locket that's appropriate for an eight-year-old. The gift, apparently, was her idea—they discussed it beforehand.

I am a thirty-two-year-old woman sitting across from my mother and she is blind. Invisibility is the thing I live in fear of. I implode, folding like origami. I try to speak but have no words. My response is primitive, before language, before cognition—the memory of the body.

Her lobster finished, she removes her plastic bib and orders another drink.

"I have to go soon," I say.

She takes out a cigarette case and extracts a long, thin cigarette.

I check my watch.

"Will you ever forgive me?"

"For what?"

"Giving you away."

"I forgive you. You absolutely did the right thing," I say, never having meant it more. "Really." I get up.

"I have to go," I say. I flee, leaving the woman in the rabbit coat alone with her Harveys Bristol Cream.

"Will I see you again?" she calls after me.

I pretend I don't hear. I don't turn around. I walk out of the restaurant and cross to the other side of the hotel; I don't breathe until I am safe on the other side.

My friend is in the Oak Bar. Several minutes pass before I am able to say anything.

"Well, what was she like?"

"I have no idea." In retrospect, I think I was in shock.

"All you all right?" the friend asks.

"I don't know."

"Tell me," she says.

Someone else, another mind, might extrapolate from her demeanor, her gestures. All I can say is, "Dusty Springfield."

"What would you have liked from her?" the friend asks.

"Literally? I would have liked it if she'd looked at me and asked, Is there anything you need, anything I can do for you, anything you want to tell me?"

"Did you make a plan to see her again?"

"No." I will never see her again. Somehow I know that.

*   *   *

On Valentine's Day the phone rings. "You can just go to the roof of your building and jump off."

"Ellen?"

"I'm angry with you, can you tell?"

"Yes."

"You didn't send me a Valentine," she says.

"I didn't know I was supposed to," I say. "I didn't send anyone a Valentine."

"Well, all you had to do was go to the store and pick one out."

"I'm not really sure why you're so angry with me."

"You don't take good care of me. You should adopt me and take good care of me," she says.

"I can't adopt you," I say.

"Why not?"

I don't know how to respond. "You're scaring me," is all I can manage.

"Are you still there?" She asks.

"Yes."

"Can you hold on while I get a drink of water?" *Water.* Her accent, her pronunciation long, a Maryland twang infused with the flavor of the Jersey Shore. Hold on while I get a drink of water. Was it water or was it Harveys Bristol Cream?

April 27, 1994, the mother's birthday. Against the advice of friends who say that following the Valentine's Day massacre I should do nothing to encourage her, I should keep my distance, I should be careful about sending mixed messages or any message at all, I feel I must do something. I want her to know that I care and am struggling with all of this, and that for the moment this is the best I can do. Not knowing the name of any florists in Atlantic City, I call FTD and try to send the very best.

"What is your name?" the woman asks. "Your name, address, and phone number?"

I give the FTD operator my name, my address, my phone, and realize that I am sweating profusely. I feel as though I am being interrogated. How many years went by when I didn't know Ellen's name, her address, her phone number?

"Yellow, pink, or red?" I am hating the operator.

"Red."

"We can deliver this tomorrow."

"No, it's for next week. I want it delivered on the twenty-seventh."

I'm ordering ahead, I want to be prepared, I don't want to miss the date.

"Deliver on the twenty-seventh," the operator says. "And the card?"

"The card?" Just asking me about the card makes me livid.

The card. " 'Happy Birthday, Ellen'—signed 'A.M.' " I can't bring myself to say "Love."

"Just 'A.M.'?" the order person asks. "Not, 'Love, A.M.'?"

"No."

"How about 'Fondly' or 'Sincerely'?" she asks.

"Yeah," I say, "you're good at this. 'Fondly.' That would be great."

"Sincerely" sounds like a business letter. "Fondly" sounds slightly authoritarian, slightly condescending, like someone trying to be warm. Later someone tells me I could have said "Warmly," but that too is flawed, like you're intentionally holding back.

"Well," the operator says, "it's for a friend, right?"

And I think about it. I think about the difference in ordering flowers for a parent—"Happy Birthday, Mom." That's clean and clear, no confusion there. I think about ordering flowers for a loved one in glee, in passion, in slight regret.

" 'Fondly' it is," the operator says. "Hold for your total."

It is more than I want to spend on a variety of levels. I hang up exhausted.

Over the summer, I am invited to meet Norman's wife— like a date with the queen, only she is also the archetypical stepmother. Norman makes the arrangements. I will meet them at the Mayflower Hotel in downtown Washington—

yet another hotel, this time one of the oldest, most historic, known as "Washington's second-best address."

I arrive early, again auditioning, always auditioning, for a role that is never clear. The hotel is crawling with Secret Service—men in blue suits and red ties talking into their lapels. The external tension, the twittery buzz, humming headsets and walkie-talkies adds a surreal edge—a peculiar psychological reality—to the situation. A bomb-sniffing dog is led past me and into the ladies' room. Maybe she really is the queen?

Norman is in the lobby, arms open, welcoming me as if this were his own home. He tells me he's sorry but his wife will be late—there was a problem with the daughter, something vaguely medical and disturbing. We exchange small talk about traffic and parking. She arrives, he goes to her, like her footman, her servant, her guilty suitor, an alley cat dragging in his bastard surprise. She is not what you would expect a queen to be—she is dowdy and dour, a short, middle-aged woman—and from the moment we say hello, it's clear that this is just a formality, that she is not interested in anything about me. She has already made up her mind.

Norman leads us not into the restaurant but into the pub that is part of the bar. We sit at a small round table, too small for a table of strangers. Norman is between us. The waitress comes. His wife orders half a sandwich and it is clear that this will be brief, this is all that any of us are getting. We each order half a sandwich and Norman has a drink.

"You seem like an awfully nice person," she says.

I nod. I am nothing if not totally polite and respectful despite what I might be feeling—which is in part fear, the need for her approval, her welcome, some stamp of acknowledgment.

"Norman would like to take you around and introduce you to people, but you know he can't," she says.

Because it will embarrass you, I am thinking—because you will have to admit what happened.

Norman is sitting between us—I am more of him than she. He says nothing.

Later he tells me, "You and my wife didn't hit it off," as though it is my responsibility.

Meanwhile I get letters from Norman's eldest son, his namesake—someone I describe as Mr. Christian Adoption. He has two children from Korea and prides himself on being a good guy, doing the right thing, telling me stories about what a great guy his (our) father is, asking if I want to see pictures of the others—playing the rebel offering to slip me contraband.

This is the boy who used to go out with Norman and Ellen. He is the one witness to it all. He was ten when everything fell apart. He thinks we have something in common—the fact that we share our father's secret—the one contradiction being that I don't *share* the secret, I *am* the secret.

Norman arranges for the three of us to have lunch at the country club near my parents' house—a club I have never been inside because my adoptive parents are so politically opposed to country clubs that the "CCC" on the flag flying outside might as well read "KKK." No blacks, no Jews, no one "other" is welcome here.

This is the world Norman lives in—faded but presumed aristocracy. The fact is, Norman is not upper class, he is overextended. (Oddly both Norman and Ellen are obsessed with class and glamour—and talk about themselves in relation to, and as though they have something in common with, figures of the 1960s like Frank Sinatra and Jackie O.)

Norman Jr., the number one son, looks nothing like his (our) father. His hair is dark, coarse, and his complexion swarthy by comparison. We drink iced tea, eat salads of iceburg lettuce and waxy tomatoes, and talk about "my people." At a certain point, I feel like a white female Martin Luther King Jr. I want to join hands and sing, "We Shall Overcome."

By that fall of 1994, the second autumn since we met, Norman still hasn't told his other children about me.

He calls. "It's Norman. I thought I'd call ya and tell ya that I have some news. I think we've sold our house and I think we're going to be moving to Florida. But I want to talk to you when you have a chance. Uh, it'll be in the next week—so will you give me a call? Thank you, doll. Bye-bye."

At least when he's in Washington I know where he is. I return the call. Someone else answers, a boy, a man— maybe my brother or a nephew. "Can I help you?" he asks.

"I'll call back."

In 1994, I write to Norman to tell him how disappointed I am that he has not done what he promised. My life has been painful enough—I have worked too hard to get where I am in the world to now be kept a secret, to be something that anyone is embarrassed about.

Norman never mentions the letter to me. I hear about it in a letter from Norman Jr.: "Whoops, I almost forgot to answer your question about your letter. . . ." He tells me that my letter was opened by mistake by Norman Sr.'s youngest son, prompting a family crisis. Norman Jr. goes on to say that it was fortunate the letter was opened, that he too was tired of the secrecy and what I said to our father was typical of what an adopted child would say to a biological father under these circumstances: "I would have written the same letter, only sooner."

We all drift—estranged.

In the middle of the winter Ellen calls—"You'd better call your father. I don't think he's going to last."

They now have more of a relationship with each other

than they do with me, the intensity of their ongoing interest a testament to the power of the attraction.

I send Norman a note; I get no answer. I don't know if he's dead or alive.

Norman Jr. writes asking if it's okay to come to a reading I'm giving in Washington. I call and tell him that I'm happy to make a plan to meet him for a drink or lunch but that I'd rather he not come to the reading. I never hear from him again.

After the millionth phone call I ask Ellen to stop calling. I am happy to exchange letters with her, but no more calls.

"What if I go to the doctor and he tells me I have twenty-four hours to live—should I call?" she asks.

"Wait twenty-five, then call," I say, half joking.

The fact is that whatever each of them is in this for has nothing to do with me—it is not about my need, my desire, and for the moment I have had enough.

In December 1997, a week before my birthday, she sends a birthday card. It's a putrid pale pink with roses, the color of femininity, of a box of sanitary napkins. I have now come to officially loathe my birthday, to live in fear of what it might bring.

Dear Daughter
This card is being sent early as I am not sure I will still be here on the 18th of December. I go to Jefferson

Hospital on December 4 for a kidney procedure. What the outcome will be I do not know. I am very scared about the whole situation. I have Chronic Renal Failure. Jefferson is in Philadelphia, PA.

Printed on the card—one of Hallmark's best—is "I remember the first time I said, 'I love you,' to your face (I meant it for the rest of you as well). You had just been born, and I thought you were the most beautiful thing on earth. And in that little face of yours, I thought I could see the future. It looked beautiful too."

I call Ellen.

"I canceled the procedure," she says, explaining that it was some sort of diagnostic kidney test and that she was scared to do it alone.

I know I am supposed to offer to go with her. But I don't. She asks if I've heard from my father; I say no. She says that he is doing well, in Florida. We talk briefly and then I find an excuse to get off the phone.

For her birthday, the following April of 1998, I send flowers—I have done this every year since she found me. This year I get no thank-you call. I call the florist to be sure that the flowers were received. I'm told that Ellen sent them back and exchanged them for a plant—she also told the florist to expect my call.

*   *   *

It is summer, 1998. I am on Long Island in a small rented house. It is early evening. I am talking to my mother when her call-waiting beeps. She is gone a long time.

"Hold on to your hat," she says, coming back onto the line. "Ellen is dead."

I am on the phone talking to my mother when she gets a call telling her that my mother is dead. It's a little too much like a Gertrude Stein line.

The woman who delivered the news was a friend of Ellen's. I call her for more information. She tells me that it was kidney disease. Ellen was in the hospital for dialysis, but apparently she checked herself out against medical advice, went home, and was found "moribund" on her sofa. *Moribund*—bound for the morgue. She tells me that Ellen's brother was notified of her death and left Ellen's body in the Atlantic City morgue for at least a day while he was at the U.S. Open in Forest Hills.

"He wasn't playing in it, was he?" a friend later asks.

How could Ellen be dead? It makes no sense. The first thing I want to do is call her, ask what's going on, and have her say, I had to do something to get your attention.

I call my lawyer and ask him to let Norman know. I don't want to break the news or deal with his reaction.

The lawyer, ever professional, reports back that Norman "appreciated the news, asked after you, and said to tell you that he'd like to talk to you whenever you're ready."

I drive to Atlantic City with no idea what to expect. The cemetery is near the airport—there's a brick billboard just outside.

Laurel Memorial Park
Atlantic City's Most Beautiful Cemetery
For Information Call . . . New Public Mausoleum
Single Graves
Family Plots
Urn Garden Niches Available

According to her friend—who didn't make it to the funeral—Ellen wanted a Jewish funeral. Instead she got a rent-a-minister in gray polyester pants presiding over a grave in the cheap part of an Atlantic City cemetery close to the airport. There are only four seats set up. Her brother, my uncle, arrives with his wife. He is wrinkled like a corn-husk doll and wears a seersucker suit. I extend a hand toward him.

"Remind me," he says, knowing full well who I am. "What's your name?"

I ask if any other relatives are buried in this cemetery.

"No," he says.

I don't tell him that I used to drive to his house, and turn the car around in his driveway, like tagging base, touch and go. I don't tell him that I used to sit outside his white brick house—his picture-perfect prosperity—and envy him his Christmas tree and his basketball hoop. And I don't tell him that his sister used to tell me how much she didn't like him.

The rented minister does his thing and I find myself nodding along, saying "Amen" to everything, and trying to make a good impression on my uncle. The grave is open, waiting, the casket next to it, unadorned. I realize that I was half expecting a large show of flowers from Norman, something in the shape of a horseshoe.

I'm thinking Ellen is in there—in that coffin, paying attention. She knows she's dead, she knows how awful it is—I remember her irreverent bursts of emotion, how she would say whatever it was she was thinking. It's depressing as hell but I'm glad I'm there, if only to be witness to this woman's life, the end of this woman's life, to make note of it.

After the funeral, I buy a map and drive around Atlantic City, going to each of the addresses on her letters in chronological order. I find one of the houses and remember a picture she sent me along with a letter saying she was one block from the ocean. It is like déjà vu—I have been here before. The house tour is a downward spiral ending in a prefabricated semidetached town house at the tag end of the street by a landfill. At each location I take photographs—I collect information, images to organize, to comfort myself.

At her last house there are tomato plants growing outside, filled with ripening fruit. Through the kitchen window I see there are still lights on inside. I see groceries on the counter, big bottles of pills, Tootsie Rolls, and Gasex tablets. There is an inhaler on the counter, some cans of Ensure, a lighter. It looks like someone lives here. I go to the front door and ring the bell—why? From her front step, using my cell phone, I dial her number and hear the phone ringing in the house; her machine picks up—her voice on the recording.

Looking through the kitchen window and into the living room, I see something green, a plant decorated with blinking out-of-season Christmas lights. Is this the plant?

What is so sad is that this is a woman who I had to protect myself from while she was alive—and now she is dead and I am doing chin-ups outside her kitchen window, scrambling for clues.

From here, I go further, I look at Atlantic City—stopping at Lucy the Elephant, a wooden turn-of-the-century tavern looking out over the ocean, a window in her ass. I park, walk out onto a fishing pier; the clouds are doing what I call the God thing, splitting light into visible rays. I see dolphins in the distance. I end up in a casino dumping quarters into slot machines. It is getting late, and although I still cannot reconcile anything, I leave with more than what I came with.

A week later, Ellen's lawyer and executor and supposed

friend, who was also curiously absent from her funeral, agrees to let me into the house. I rent a car, bring some boxes, some plastic bags, and two of my friends for support.

"I don't know what kind of relationship you had," the lawyer says as he's unlocking her door. "But I didn't find much, just a few pictures. My wife and I went through it. She's an antiques dealer, she said there's nothing."

The house has been ransacked—there are candles but no candlesticks, plates but no silverware, and the copper pots and pans I saw through the kitchen window are gone. The lawyer tells me that he and his wife have been organizing things, getting ready for a tag sale. Cleared of anything of material value, the house is still filled with stuff. There is the crocheted afghan that covered the sofa where she was found, lots of ugly candy dishes, weird plastic dolls with music-box bases, supplies from the failed beauty shop she opened a few years before, Christmas decorations. And there is a small blue vanity case—the kind of thing you'd see in a movie, Audrey Hepburn or Barbra Streisand carrying it through the airport, a bellhop following with all the other, larger bags. The case has a built-in combination lock and the latch was open—clearly someone had already looked through it. It is filled with the debris, crumbs of a life lived—encrusted with old makeup, bobby pins, a hair roller, a long-expired ring of birth control pills, loose coins. Either she or someone she knew was king of the silver dollar, because they're everywhere, in every drawer of the dresser. The suitcase sums her up—it wouldn't have surprised me to find pieces of Lego in there or parts of a broken toy. It was, on the one hand, a sophisticated piece of luggage, and yet its condition gave the appearance of having been used by a child, a girl playing an adult. I leave it behind—it's too much, too intimate, like taking her toothbrush from its cup.

I go through the house, randomly putting things in boxes, my two friends trailing—asking what I want to keep, what I'm looking for. I am wandering, opening and closing closet doors, having no idea how to add it all up. Devastating, depressing—this was the sum of her life. On the inside the house feels impermanent, occupied by a transient, someone not living in the house but on it, like a squatter. It's messy, as though a hurricane has blown through, and there's no way of knowing if that was her or if someone had gone through it like a pirate, looting. There is nothing of substance—and I don't mean value but solidity. Everything feels like it is made of paper, like it could crumble and blow away. The lawyer lets us into the house—and then about twenty minutes later he finds me and asks, "Will you be done in fifteen minutes?"

My friend takes him aside and says, "Look, this is her mother, this is as close as she's ever been to her mother, so just give her a moment—if you have things to do, come back in an hour or so."

I shoot photographs of everything, knowing this is it, the one time, the only time, the last time, and I have to try and capture what I can. I have to find a way to save it for later because I can't deal with it in the moment. I photograph her bedroom and the things in her bedroom—closet, headboard (brass but unattached and leaning sharply forward). I photograph the top of her dresser—Excedrin, Johnson's Baby Powder, perfume, candy, a China geisha, a bowl of loose change, and a stack of baseball cards! I photograph the insides of her dresser drawers—each stuffed with unfolded clothing—a lifetime supply of lingerie. I take pictures of her bathroom—thirty-two Chanel lipsticks and dozens of the strange little dolls that are all over the house, six-inches tall and dressed like colonial ladies, in wide skirts, with ruffles and, on their heads, lace hats, orange hair, and weirdly red, clown noses and circus makeup. I photograph the back of the bathroom door—her bathrobe and multiple shower caps. I photograph the other two empty bedrooms, filled with boxes, with stuff she'd clearly brought from the last place, cartons and shopping bags, wrapping paper, shoes still in their boxes. In a corner of the kitchen there is a menorah and then, just behind it, a crucifix, and in front a framed photograph of a dog. I use a half dozen disposable cameras, and when they are done I put the cameras in the boxes.

*　　*　　*

In the front closet, I find a fur: a stole, with her initials sewn into the underside in pink script. I imagine it was among her prized possessions, that Norman gave it to her. A luxury. It must have seemed glamorous when she got it. Now it looks old, mangy. I leave it hanging.

I take pieces of paper; boxes of paper, among them a receipt for a diamond ring from 1963; an old packet of what look like birth control pills, an arrest warrant, a package from Saks that must have arrived recently, two pairs of rubbery "slimming" underwear with the tags still on, one in black, one in flesh color. What size was she? A brown cashmere sweater exactly like the cream one Norman sent me for Christmas the first year we were in touch—the infamous cashmere sweater. In her bedroom her pants are hung over a chair, black jeans, not unlike the black jeans I often wear. They still hold the creases of her body. I put my hand in the pocket; there is a wad of money, loose bills, a pack of gum. This is exactly the way I keep my money. It's the one thing my mother is always on me about: How can you keep your money like that? No one keeps their money like that—don't you want to keep it in a purse? The wad is thick, jammed down into the bottom of the pocket—how many women in their early sixties keep money in a wad in their pocket? It creeps me out, this indescribable subtlety of biology. In her pockets I find the same things I find in mine.

I am reading a pile of clothes, a messy house, looking for information, clues.

I remember the writer James Ellroy talking to me about his mother's clothing—getting his murdered mother's clothing out of the police evidence room—years after the fact. He talked about taking the clothing out of the sealed plastic bags and wanting to smell it, wanting to rub his face with it.

There is a tendency to romanticize the missing person—to think about her is to allow her in. I hear her voice in my head—unreliable though she was, she is the only one who could explain to me what happened.

When I leave, I put four boxes of assorted paper into the rented car. I have no idea what I've taken, what it might add up to. I drive my two friends into downtown Atlantic City and take them out for dinner at one of the casinos. I feel indebted—I couldn't have gotten through the day without them. The setting is surreal, a faux underwater ice palace. We sit staring at the slowly melting sea-creature ice sculptures surrounding us. The lighting constantly shifts, green and purple and blue—like Jacques Cousteau on acid. The three of us order the same thing—steak and baked potatoes; it's as though we need a good meal to ground us. We are silent, stunned—it's hard to know what to say after a day like this. In the end Ellen pays for the meal. I use the wad of money from her black pants, and whatever is left I leave as a tip.

That night in New York, I clean my apartment. Frantically, hysterically, I go through everything, throwing things out—I have shower caps from every hotel I ever stayed in, soaps, shampoo. I have everything that she had. I throw it all away. I cannot be like Ellen—it can't all happen again the same way.

I think of the flowers she had turned into a plant, the plant I saw through the kitchen window, the plant with the Christmas tree lights turned on, and me, a Christmas baby, the thing that couldn't be forgotten—did she leave the lights on for me?

I struggle with how to narrate the confusion, the profound loss of a piece of myself that I never knew, a piece that I pushed away because it was so frightening.

The autobiography of the unknown.

A couple of months later, I call Norman—he says, "Let me call you right back." It's the first time we've spoken since Ellen's death. He tells me that he saw Ellen in Washington not long before she died. I have no idea if this was the first time they'd seen each other in almost forty years or if they'd been seeing each other repeatedly since their independent reunions with me. He tells me that he knew she was sick. The doctor had told her that she needed a kidney, and according to Norman, Ellen wanted him to ask me for one. He becomes adamant; she asked him and he said no. He told her that they couldn't ask me for any favors, on account of how neither of them had ever done anything for me. He tells me he offered his own kidney—that he called his doctor and asked about it. I believe he asked his doctor something about it but beyond that it seems unlikely. We're talking on his car phone because he's afraid to talk to me from his home phone, but he expects me to believe that he could give Ellen a kidney—would he tell his wife, his children? I believe that when Ellen asked Norman, he said no at first and then agreed to ask me and told Ellen that I'd turned her down. That would explain a lot. It would explain why I didn't hear from her before she died.

When I speak to Norman, I get emotional and think, Oh no, I'm reminding him of *her*. I tell Norman that I've had enough, that I can't do this again, that I don't want one day to get a phone call summoning me to another church, where I'll stand in the back, unwelcome, and witness friends and family mourning the passing of a man I never really knew but was somehow a part of.

"I understand," he says. "Call me. Call me in the car. My wife isn't in the car very often—we can talk."

"I'm not your mistress. I'm your daughter. And I'm not calling you in your car," I say.

"Fine thing," he replies.

Book Two

Unpacking My Mother

Ellen Ballman

t is seven years before I can open the boxes I took from Ellen's house. It is 2005, and I am still on the same page, I am still wondering exactly what happened.

"Moribund on the sofa"—what did that mean? Half dead, already dead, well on the way to being dead? Was she in a coma? Did she know someone had come for her? Did she hope to be saved? How does someone live to be sixty and end up so alone? I go through the few papers I have—her death certificate says she died at 3 A.M. in the emergency room of the hospital. Who called the ambulance? How long was she in the emergency room? She must have been a little bit alive when she got there, other-wise the DOA box would have been checked. I think of calling Atlantic City 911 and asking for a transcription. And why am I remembering someone saying something about her being discovered by a Chinese deliveryman?

Seven years after the fact and it is as fresh as when it happened. It seems that this is the nature of trauma—it doesn't change, soften, go dim, mutate into something less sharp, less dangerous.

Even now I want to call Ellen and ask what it was all about. Did she kill herself? Sort of. She chose to check herself out of the hospital against medical advice and went home to die alone on her sofa. Her fear of fear, her dislike of doctors, her underlying anxiety were certainly con-tributing factors.

I remember the birthday card—"This card is being sent early as I am not sure I will still be here on the 18th of De-cember. I go to Jefferson Hospital on December 4 for a kid-ney procedure. What the outcome will be I do not know."

I remember calling Ellen, half annoyed, half concerned.

"I canceled the procedure," she said.

I never understood what the procedure was for; the closest thing I got to an answer was something about blood flow to a kidney and that she'd seen a lot of doctors—including one in Atlantic City who sent her to someone in Philadelphia—but she was scared to have anything done down there, to be alone in the hospital, and I knew I was supposed to say, I'll come and take care of you.

Part of me thinks that if she'd asked in the "right way," I would have helped her, and I am annoyed with myself. What does it matter how she tried to ask? She was afraid and she'd probably never gotten good results with asking—probably in part because she didn't know how. So instead of getting what she wanted, she continually got what she didn't—she pushed people away.

And I cannot escape the nearly biblical connection of the kidney—I was adopted into my family on account of my mother's son Bruce dying of kidney failure. Is it my fault that she died? Was I expected to give her a kidney? Just after her death, I called her doctor in Atlantic City; in death I was to her what I couldn't be in life. "This is Ellen Ballman's daughter, I'm looking for some information." I paused, waiting for him to say, "Ellen Ballman was unmarried and had no children. I have no idea who you are."

"A transplant would have saved her," he said, without prejudice. There was nothing in his voice implying that it should have come from me. Without prompting he went on to say that the kidney she needed would not necessarily have to have been my kidney. Had they talked about it— did he know *who* I was? Had he asked her, Do you have a family?

"I don't know why she checked herself out of the hospital. I don't know what she was thinking. Her condition was treatable—she could have been saved."

After she died I wrote letters—to the brief list of friends her lawyer gave me, to the friend who called to say she was dead, to her niece in California, and so on. I wrote to them, telling them who I was and that I would very much like to hear more about Ellen, their memories, experiences, anything they wanted to share. I dropped the letters in the mail and nothing happened. The only person I heard from was Ellen's Polish cleaning lady—who didn't speak English. The woman she worked for on Tuesdays called me and together they left a message on my answering machine. It was a message left in translation as relayed by her Tuesday employer—the cleaning lady is heartbroken, she loved Ellen, she had no idea she was so sick. The cleaning lady had gone to Poland to visit her family; "she was away but now she is back." I should call her anytime. I should come visit. She loves me very much. The Tuesday employer also left her name and phone number— "Call anytime," she said. I couldn't bring myself to call.

It is human nature to run from danger—but why did I have to be so human? Why could I not have been more capable, a better biological daughter? Why did I not have the strength and perspective to both protect myself *and* give? I failed her—I was so busy protecting myself from her that I didn't do a good enough job recognizing the trouble she was in. I expected her to ask for what she needed in the way that I thought was appropriate. I could not see her selfishness with perspective, could not see that this was a woman in enormous pain, could not escape myself, my own needs, my own trapped desire. What does it matter how she asked? I should have given. I should have given despite not wanting to give. And what self was I protecting—does bracing oneself against something offer any protection?

People tell me how to feel. "You must be relieved," they say. "You must be confused." "You must be ambivalent."

I failed her. I didn't pay enough attention to the last letters, to the last time we spoke. She had called telling me to "hurry up and call your father, he may not last long."

The idea that she was calling about him, that she and he had a relationship that extended beyond me, was galling. And that he was my father and had made me prove it, only to then not talk to me, and now I should hurry and call because he may not last—that these people who had so suddenly arrived might now so suddenly disappear was all too much.

My mother is dead. My mother called to tell me my mother is dead? This is the dissonance, the split, the impossibility of living two lives at once.

*   *   *

Yom Kippur, autumn, 1998. I am in Saratoga Springs, New York, at Yaddo, an artists' colony. It is just a few weeks after the funeral. I go to services hosted by the local temple. I am alone among strangers, in a place safe for grief, and for me this is the memorial—"May he remember." There is a part of the Yom Kippur service called the Yizkor—during which they read the names of all those related to the congregation who have died that year. I add her name to that list. The names are read aloud. There are other names before and after hers. Her name is called out, it is heard—equal to the others, it is not alone. Her name is said aloud, it is offered to everyone. I see other people crying and feel that I have done something, I have given her one thing she wanted, to be recognized, to be noticed. This is her Jewish funeral. I am holding a memorial service for a mother I never knew in a room full of strangers. We are embracing history and grief and all that has come and gone, and it makes more sense than anything has.

I am thinking about Atlantic City and walking out on the pier and how the clouds cracked open and rays of late-afternoon rainbow-colored light came streaming down. I am thinking about the time I sent her rose petals from the Yaddo garden. I am thinking of how she wanted everything and anything and how insatiable she was. I am glad I am there, alone, among strangers. I cry throughout the service. I am crying not just for her, but for myself, for every accident that has been a part of this, for every failing on everyone's part, for the damned fragility of being human, for being afraid, ashamed. This is my atonement; I am confessing my sins, beating my chest, asking for forgiveness for what I have said and for what I have not said, for what I have done and for what I have not done, for those I have hurt or offended knowingly or unknowingly, for my errors of omission—this confession is known in Judaism as the Viduy. I am crying for how isolated I am, how alone, and how I have to go through life like this.

Did I ever say how precariously positioned I feel—on the edge of the earth, as though my permit could be revoked at any second?

The boxes. I come home from Yaddo and the boxes are in my apartment waiting for me, greeting me, nudging me to remember what I can't forget. I cannot open the boxes. I am afraid of them, as though they contain something that might hurt me. Peeling the tape off them might unleash a virulent bacteria, just touching them might somehow infect me with *her*. I live with them like furniture, taking care to steer around them, to not let anything I care about come in contact with them, and then finally, more than nine months later, I put them in storage. I banish the boxes to the netherland of ministorage—before they go I mark them carefully in Sharpie marker on all sides, *Dead Ellen* 1–4. She put me up for adoption—I'm sending her to ministorage. She will join my tax records, my vinyl record collection, my dot matrix printer, my old typewriter, becoming a piece of my life I am unwilling to entirely unload but that is best kept off-site.

What is the half-life of a toxic box? When will I be ready to look inside—does the potential to rattle and shake lessen over time?

In the spring of 2005 I promise myself to once and for all deal with dead Ellen. I bring the boxes out of suspension, deliver them back to my apartment. Over time they have ripened; there is a certain smell to them—active disintegration. And again they sit, linger, become furniture. I stack things on top of them: suitcases, books, things of great weight. I am covertly holding them closed.

In the fall of 2005, twelve years after she found me, I take the boxes with me to Long Island for a weekend—just me and the four corrugated cardboard containers of dead Ellen. I take the boxes to the same small house where I stood in the yard and listened as my mother told me that my mother was dead. The house, then a rental, now is mine—a piece of something people call home. I take four boxes to the house on Long Island, a safe and controlled place—where like a bomb squad I plan to detonate them. I put the boxes on the kitchen table—my grandmother's table. There is no escaping them now, no way around it.

I ask my family to stay home. I cannot do this with an audience, I have to be alone, able to sit with whatever I find. I need to not have to explain what can't be explained—all that I am now of course trying to explain. I sit before the boxes, preparing to take inventory, giddy like a child playing the game of going through the mother's purse, and then also feeling a more serious weight—I am the guardian, the keeper of what remains, and if I was not able to know her in life, perhaps I can crawl closer in death. Is there such a thing as intimacy after the fact? Will I find her in these boxes, will I know her any better after I am done? There is a piece of me that wishes I had taken more—perhaps if I'd taken ten boxes there'd be more of something, not just more of the same.

Box 1—the item on top is sheet music. "Hail to the Redskins." I don't know exactly why I was so surprised that this was the first item—was it because my biological father was a college football player, or that I could all too easily picture the two of them going to Redskins games while his wife was home with the kids? But it was especially interesting in light of other information I discovered: Ellen's 1971 arrest for gambling—setting up a gaming table in the Sheraton Park Hotel and taking bets during a Cowboys-Redskins game—and an antitrust lawsuit that my father filed against the Redskins and pro football when he wanted to bring a new football team to town and ran into difficulty. And as soon as I see the sheet music, I also see myself at thirteen with braces in my bedroom in my parents' house in Chevy Chase and my clarinet teacher, Mr. Schreiber, sitting beside me while I honked and screeched, stopping to lick the reed of my rented clarinet, wanting to get it right. Mr. Schreiber was the leader of the Redskins marching band—the Indian chief—who with a long head-dress over his thick white hair would lead the band out onto the field at halftime.

Under the sheet music is a faux leather portfolio of photographs. I reflexively take a deep breath—preparing for what comes next—but on account of the dust, I have a coughing fit and have to go get a drink. The photos are the work of Harris & Ewing—the largest photo studio in Washington, photographers of presidents and high society—and apparently several are of my mother as an infant. In the first two portraits she is about four months old—there's one serious, one smiling—and then she is somewhere near two, in a white dress with a big bow in her hair, white lace-up shoes, delicate and delighted—again and always looking off to the side. And then a little older, maybe three or four, posing with a big beautiful Dalmatian. And again—maybe part of the same shoot—in lederhosen or a pinafore. There is the palpable sense of her as Daddy's little girl—devilish glimmer in the eye, she is shy and she is charming and she is defiant—and I have the strange sense that she knows more than she is able to fully understand. She is not a baby but a girl, and still and always there is a tentativeness and a need for confirmation—one can see it all. And for me there is a dull familiarity, an inescapable, unnamable relatedness—we do not look alike but in common. There is something similar in the arms, in the cheeks and the eyes—we have the same eyes.

There is a Harris & Ewing portrait of Ellen's mother—cool, crisp, cold, proud of herself if no one else. The fact that these photos exist at all speaks to a certain kind of prosperity. The average person in the early 1940s did not have portraits taken of themselves and their children. It also reminds me of something Ellen once said to me—"Let's have our portrait painted." When she said it, the words seemed to exist in another world. Did she once have her portrait painted? Was it something promised that never happened? There is another photo taken on board a ship by someone else, of Ellen's mother and a woman I assume is her mother's mother, Mary Hannan—sometime in the 1930s. And then there is another of Mary Hannan long ago—a youthful, beautiful young woman.

Mixed between the pages there are random snapshots—Ellen playing on the beach, with her brother deep in the background. There is one that I assume is her father and brother in the backyard of their house. And then Ellen at about seven or eight standing outside the house with her brother—he is in his military school uniform, fists clenched at his side, his mother the photographer's shadow a dark outline on the sidewalk—and by now her father is gone. And then Ellen is on a sofa next to her mother—adolescent, chubby, and excruciatingly uncomfortable. The images are frozen moments of family relation; they are documents taken to serve as proof and memory when there is no longer anyone to tell the story.

Things fall out—dozens of unopened bills with the yellow forwarding stickers from the post office, *Notify Sender of New Address*. Hers was a life lived in motion, spiraling down, running, barely one step ahead of herself. Envelopes slip to the floor—insurance overdue notice of $530 and another from a collection agency for $13,043.75 due to the office of comptroller of revenue. There is a set of legal papers relating to the reopening of a case filed by a family on behalf of their children to recover damages suffered by lead paint poisoning in buildings owned and managed by the defendants—specifically and especially *Ellen Ballman*.

There is a letter from Security National Bank: "This is to advise you that because of an unsatisfactory relationship on your account, we must request the account be closed within 15 days of this letter." There is a commercial gas and electric bill due for over $10,000. And an envelope with an autumn 1995 Mark, Fore & Strike catalog, *Fun Casual Clothing Since 1951*. The odor wafting up from the box stings—it's a little mothball, a little hamster cage, a little asthmatic, and definitely something turned sour. There's a letter from the Maryland Department of Public Works dated June 6, 1984, a citation for general nuisance, vacant lot conditions, overgrowth of tall weeds and brush, scattered bottles, cans, and paper, a rat running along the front of the lot. The address, 4709 Langedrum Lane, Chevy Chase, Maryland. It is a few miles from where I grew up—and a place not known for rats. There is a notice of cancelation of insurance and another notice for delinquent taxes on a property on Seventh Street in Washington, D.C.

Under the photographs and all through the boxes there are notes, scraps of paper with little rhyming poems scrawled in pencil and pen and always signed "JC" (Jack). Who was he to her—a lover, an old friend, a friend of her father's? I know from my research that he was arrested more than once for gambling, that he owned a dry cleaning store and later lived in Atlantic City. And I know how sad Ellen was when he was ill and after he died. How did they meet? He had a wife, Katherine—I see her name on some of the documents and I find a card from her to Ellen. Clearly, he cared a great deal about Ellen—he once wrote me a letter, attesting to the validity of Ellen's stories about her mother.

The boxes are like a paper trail version of *This Is Your Life*. Inside one of the boxes is a smaller box marked *Master Bedroom*. I peel cracked cellophane tape off. Inside is an open metal file—in each compartment a manila folder, each folder trouble, a case in and of itself, literally. The rack is filled with file after file of real estate transactions gone wrong, buildings bought and sold, backup loans, trusts, deeds, dozens of letters to lawyers, lots of back-and-forth, motions to counter, depositions. Motion for leave to withdraw as counsel for plaintiff and for counterdefendant. There is nothing about this that is good news. At the back there is an old telephone message book—with duplicates. *Call Rudy at work. Ms. Watson—important. Re Rose, verification was sent on wife last week. For Alex, re Lackey could he come by at 3pm today?* It's been years but I feel like returning the calls. Hi there, can you tell me about Ellen Ballman? How did you get to know her? Was she nice? Was she fair? Was she a good person? And then there is yet another file with a note on top. *Please talk to Ellen about this! She's annoying me to death about it. What does she want me to do except bring it to your attention!!!* There is a piece of paper—on which someone has scrawled "For Your Information" and a notation that looks like "EB hours 300 as of 8-8-89." (I take this to mean she has served three hundred hours of community service so far, but I could be wrong—maybe she had three hundred to go.) It is attached to a document that reads:

IN THE CIRCUIT COURT FOR MONTGOMERY
COUNTY MARYLAND
Criminal No *****

Upon consideration of Defendant's Motion for
Modification or Reduction of Sentence, the

State having deferred to the Court's ruling,
and verification having been received that ——————
has completed the terms of her probation, it
is . . .

ORDERED, that the guilty finding against the
Defendant in this case be, and the same hereby
is, STRICKEN, and it is further ORDERED, that
a disposition of Probation before Judgment under article 27, Section 641 be entered, and it
is further ORDERED that supervised probation
be, and the same hereby is TERMINATED, and case
closed, and it is further ORDERED, that the
hearing scheduled for August 5, 1989 be re-
moved from the Court's calendar.

I do not think that the above pertained to Ellen. I
think it pertained to the woman who was sentenced along
with her, and was sent to Ellen to prompt her to complete
her community service. Curiously, the woman who was
sentenced along with her was the same woman who called
my mother to tell her—us—that Ellen was dead.

There are pharmacy receipts. I jot down the names of the
drugs and make a note to look them up. Meprobamate, for
short-term relief of the symptoms of anxiety. Tenormin, a
beta blocker used to treat high blood pressure and angina
pectoris. It is also used after a heart attack to improve sur-
vival. Dyazide, a potassium sparing and thiazide diuretic
used to treat high blood pressure and swelling due to

excess body water. Wygesic, an analgesic combination used to relieve pain. Premarin—conjugated estrogens used to reduce menopause symptoms. Imipramine, a tricyclic anti-depressant used to treat depression.

Just going through the list gives me chest pains. Maybe her father really did die of a heart attack—her maternal grandfather did at age fifty-three. Whatever was going on, it sounds complicated by her emotional state—did she have high blood pressure, did she have a heart condition? "It was all those damn diet pills," my father said. "No matter what they said to her she wouldn't stop taking the diet pills." She was depressed, anxious, and dying when she checked herself out of the hospital, and she could have been saved.

Does any of this come as a shock? Not really. Among the first facts I had about my mother came from the private investigator—interestingly, an adopted woman who had never searched for her own family—who said, "In a nutshell she was indicted and driven out of town." I never knew exactly what she was talking about, but it's starting to make sense. I find articles about Ellen in the *Washington Post*—stories about her business practices, which amounted to her and a friend running a "chop shop" for documents in which they changed people's income records, forged tax documents, and without customers' knowledge qualified them for loans in excess of what they would otherwise be allowed to borrow. In court she admitted to falsifying documents for mortgages worth tens of millions of dollars and was sentenced to an eighteen-month suspended prison term, three years' probation, and ordered to perform five hundred hours of community service.

What was surprising to me was how it all seemed to go on and on for years and years. The arrest and conviction were just the last straw. Not everything she did was illegal, but even that which wasn't was done in the most difficult way possible—there was no grace. Did she plan these things? Was she scheming all along? Did she have a pathological need to make a deal, to do business in a certain way? Did she just not know how to do it the right way? It would seem that to do anything the way it was supposed to be done was fundamentally against her grain. There are times I think maybe she was a sort of Robin Hood and it's okay, and then I think not. The possibility that it is pathological makes me want to know more about her father. I write to the FBI and request his FBI file under the Freedom of Information Act, only to find out that it was destroyed on schedule in 1971 according to government rules pertaining to document storage. But at least it confirms something—there was a file.

My mother as a kind of Bonnie and Clyde—always on the run, a Bonnie on her own always looking for Clyde, always looking for her father. And just as one worries about a genetic predisposition to a heart attack, I worry about a genetic predisposition to gambling, to midlife disaster. Will

I suddenly become a criminal? I think about her in relation to the father—he too had midlife career disaster, not exactly criminal but certainly unbecoming. The bank he was president of went under largely due to a kind of good-old-boy mismanagement—the bank's board favored loans to officers, directors, and their relatives above a responsibility to customers. I wonder if it was some sense of themselves as exempt from the rules that brought them together. Were they clever and crafty together? Did they take pleasure in their outlaw status—did they think they would somehow get away with it—what ever that might have meant? I think of Ellen in middle age—a woman with physical and emotional problems, cobbling it together, living alone in a kind of postmodern version of the Atlantic City portrayed in Louis Malle's brilliant 1981 film.

And in the end, almost after the fact, I find an unopened letter from the Hebrew Home of Greater Washington in Rockville, Maryland, dated March 29, 1989. I open the letter, "There are no words which can fully express my sincere appreciation for your most generous gifts to the Hebrew Home. The Computers will allow us to do our work more effectively and ultimately, the residents of the Home will benefit." The letter goes on to acknowledge the donation of four computers, five monitors, five keyboards, and a printer. I find myself wondering if this is a Robin Hood moment—all the more compelling because the letter was never opened.

*   *   *

There are no pictures of her at seventeen—the age when my father asked her to marry him. No pictures of her at twenty-two, pregnant with me, no pictures of her in the hospital—holding me, dressing me in my "going-home" outfit. Do those pictures exist, were they in some other box I didn't find? What did she dress like in the 1950s, when she worked for my father at the Princess Shop? After all, that was the time of the French designer knockoff—Dior's A-line, Givenchy's sack, the boxy Chanel jacket, the swing coat, perfect for hiding a pregnancy. Did she like the new "modern" materials, nylon, Crimplene, and Orlon? Did she wear cone bras or all-in-one girdles? Was she the kind of teenager who dressed like an adult, or was she wearing poodle skirts, bobby sox, and going to drive-in movies? What was she thinking? This was the era of atomic anxiety, of Perry Como, Dean Martin, Connie Francis, and the beehive hairdo. It was the time of air-raid sirens and fallout shelters, the Rosenberg electrocutions and the McCarthy hearings. This was Washington, D.C., in the 1950s—and it was prime time for my mother.

I had hoped to find her in these boxes, to find a description of her childhood, the games she had played, clues to her troubled relationship with her mother and what she really knew about her father, her memories, the trinkets that she kept as talismans to protect or guide her. I hoped to have some idea of how she saw herself, what her hopes and dreams had been. I wanted to know her secrets.

I take the empty boxes to the dump, crack them in half, and toss them into the recycling bin—I am sending dead Ellen around once more. Maybe she'll come back as napkins or paper or some kind of shopping bag. I hurl the old metal file into one of the bins. It lands hard, the sound exploding like a grenade—everyone turns and looks. I shrug. I throw away the old mail, the scraps of paper, the bits and pieces, keeping enough to fill one box—a box to remind me. I put the box in the car and drive it back to New York, where it waits in a corner of my apartment, and then once again gets sent to ministorage.

It is 2005 and all I can think is that this is not how the woman who was so concerned about appearances would want to have been seen, this is not how the woman with thirty-two Chanel lipsticks would want to have been presented—but this is who she is and what she left behind.

Imagining my mother.

I think of my mother and imagine a young woman who hoped for more. I think of my mother and try to inhabit her experience.

In the 1950s ladies still wore hats and gloves and men wore overcoats. Young men and women met at socials, or-

ganized dances, chaperoned. The men hoped to go to college; the women hoped.

At Catholic school the nuns told Ellen very little about
the birds and the bees and a lot about sin and all that could
go wrong. Almost everything already had gone wrong for
Ellen, but no one acknowledged that. She was surrounded
by people who didn't want to know, and quickly learned
that faith got her nothing—in fact her belief that something would save her got her into trouble. At Catholic
school she protected herself by insisting—at least to
herself—that she was Jewish. Her mother was Catholic,
her father was Jewish, and she always described herself
as her father's little girl.

Pin money. Her mother didn't have much—whatever
she had she got from her new husband, and she didn't
want to share. Ellen got a job working in the dress shop—
one night, weekends, and holidays, and a good discount.
She liked working, liked acting like a grown-up—helping
the ladies with their shopping. They treated her in the
motherly sort of way that she wished her own mother
would.

Ellen opened a bank account—vowing to save half, or
at least part, of what she earned. She had a future. The
boss offered her a ride home—she accepted. In the car
they talked. Again, her boss offered her a ride home, she
accepted, and he asked if she wanted to go out for dinner.

And then again her boss offered her a ride, took her out to dinner, and after dinner they parked the car somewhere where they could talk. She asked him about what he hoped to be, what dreams he had—he found that appealing. He appeared interested in her—she found that appealing. She was practicing on him—being girlish and tempting. He took it as an opportunity. Imagine the fumbling. He wants it but doesn't want to say what *it* is; she doesn't want *it* but has no idea how to set a limit.

Where did it start—in a car, in a hotel, in the back of the store, in a borrowed place? What did he say to her? Did he believe it himself, did she believe him? How often did it happen? Does he think he's stealing something— sampling something he shouldn't? What part of her is his favorite? Imagine her newly formed figure, fresh, tender, perfect. Imagine him. Does she worry about getting pregnant—does she even know how girls get pregnant? Does he worry about it?

This is their courtship; she is waiting, she is waiting for him, she is waiting while he is at work, while he is with his family. While she is waiting she does mischievous things; she tells her friends, she makes sure her mother finds out, she thinks there is cachet in the fact that she is the younger girl of a much older man. She wants something else, something more—more than she wants him—but what she gets is sex, and then he's gone. He has her in ways his wife

would never allow, gets from her things he would otherwise never think to ask.

They go for drinks—martinis, gimlets, or Tom
Collinses, mai tais, Singapore slings, and sea breezes.
They snack on salty cocktail nuts and have prime rib and
salad of iceberg lettuce with Maytag blue cheese dressing.

He offers to set her up in a place of her own—she's
thinking they're setting up house, he's thinking it's a place
to be alone with her. She's thinking it's a way out, an escape from her mother—and her mother's husband. She ac-
cepts defiantly, half in anger, half wishing her mother
could stop her—knowing she will not allow herself to be
stopped.

At seventeen she is the boss of herself; she is glad to be
getting out from under her mother's coldness, the years
of opposition, out from under the eye and hand of her
stepfather.

"He's nice to me—he cares about me," she tells her
mother.

"He doesn't care about you—married men don't care
about girls like you," her mother says.

"He's getting an apartment for us."

"He's never going to leave his wife."

"He's going to marry me."

"He's already married."

She starts to pack a suitcase.

"There is something wrong with you," her mother says.

"You are what's wrong with me," Ellen says.

"I would send you to boarding school, but now that you're ruined the nuns won't take you—no one wants used goods."

Her mother grabs the suitcase. "It's my suitcase, I never said you could use it."

Ellen gets paper bags, grocery sacks from the kitchen. She packs her clothes in the paper bags. Her mother goes through her dresser drawers throwing things at her. Ellen goes into the attic and finds an old traveling bag that had been her father's—later she finds a dead mouse in it, a shriveled furry husk. She stuffs her bags with clothing, with the trinkets from the top of her dresser, with the stuffed animals her father gave her long ago. She goes out to the door.

"If you go out that door, don't think you're ever coming back," her mother yells after her.

He is not waiting for her outside—he is afraid of her mother. He is down the street, around the corner. She toddles off, dropping things on the sidewalk as she goes.

The apartment is in a big building on Connecticut Avenue, a small one-bedroom in the back, with a view of another apartment. It is "furnished."

Whose furniture was it? The woman who lived there

before—who finally got married, who took a job in Ohio, who went home to live with her mother, who died lonely of old age at forty. Whose was it really? It was a little of this and that, what people left behind, what no one wanted.

They have fun together—he is able to play with her, to joke and push in a way that he has never been able to before. He has always been the one teased. She tolerates it because it is familiar, and she gives it back to him and then some. He teaches her to drive—he teases her, she gets mad, and he laughs all the more.

When he is not there, she sleeps with the stuffed animals she brought from home.

It is incredibly quiet. She has a radio and then a secondhand television set, and later a phone. There are a few mismatched dishes in the kitchen cabinets, things he's taken from his mother's basement, telling her it's for the kids to play with or needed at the house. There are crocheted rugs on the floor—all of it is a little nubbly, a little dark and depressing, an echo of World War II, but she gets plants and sometimes she gets flowers and she feels like a grown-up, a woman with a home of her own. She sleeps with the light on. If she has one of her high school girlfriends over—they lie and say they are going to someone else's house—they roast marshmallows on the gas stove, eat candy for dinner, and go to the movies and drink coffee for breakfast. There are other times when she goes to a friend's house—and is reminded of what most girls/other girls are doing, living at home with their mothers and fathers, eating dinner in the dining room, wearing clothing that is washed and ironed for them, feeling protected. The mothers feel sorry for her and worry that she might be a bad influence. She walks to the zoo, she takes the bus downtown, and she works in the clothing store.

He and she are a good match, except that he is already married and is not going to divorce his wife, and she is already emotionally on edge. They are two people who lost their childhoods, two whose parents abandoned them to one degree or another, two people a little bit lost. I see her entertaining him, tempting and teasing him. I see him as being fatherly and calming and temperate, and I see the two of them having drinks and going wild. I see him excusing himself, washing up, and going home. I see her being angry and taking it out on him—she is dramatic and an actress.

I see her in cashmere sweaters. I see her body, new and fresh and entirely unmarked. I see her and him simultaneously discovering themselves. I see them going out on the town. I see a certain amount of swagger and bravado.

And sometimes he doesn't have time—his wife needs him, his kids need him. Sometimes he brings one of the kids. His oldest boy waits in the living room while they talk privately for a few minutes in the bedroom; the talking involves giggling and sighing. And then he tells her he can't do it anymore, it's too hard on his family. He tells her he means it this time.

She cries. She thinks she will die. She is sure she will die, she feels sick, and she feels pain in her chest. She is up all night. She drinks. She calls a friend of his, his buddy—she cannot bear to be alone.

He returns, promising that soon he will be hers completely. She pretends she is not going to take him back—she pretends she has fallen for his friend. The friend gives her some money—he also gives her something that itches.

She is lonely. She goes out at cocktail hour, to get back at him, to remind him that she is alone and he is married with children. Men buy her drinks, sometimes they buy her dinner. He is irate. He is trying to be in two places at the same time. His wife has found out. She tells him that the girl can't work at the store anymore.

When she is alone, she eats peanut butter and jelly sandwiches and drinks the liquor he has left behind. At night, when she's sleeping, she sometimes hears the sound of the men who brought her father home—she hears their voices, their footsteps. She remembers being asleep when it happened, waking up, being afraid to open the door. She remembers looking through the keyhole—seeing her father's arm hanging limp. She remembers being terrified.

His wife has told him to stop. He has told his wife that

it is over and done—he tells Ellen that it is over and done. He sneaks around. He is angry with both of them for wanting so much—for wanting more, wanting it all.

There are times she wants to leave him. She tells him she has met someone new—it is a little bit true. She tries, she attempts to replace him, but it never lasts long. She spends time with friends of his—maybe they have wives, maybe not. Once she spent the night with a friend and his wife.

I picture Norman furious and jealous.

She and his wife are at the same holiday party—they see each other across the room, they know who they are. He is there with his wife, and he ignores Ellen—or tries to. She drinks too much and throws up on the new sea green carpet in the dining room. Someone has to drive her home.

"What was she doing there?"

"She was invited."

"She should know better."

"He should know better."

Red faced.

What is she thinking? She wants to be a little girl, she wants to be taken care of, loved—she thinks his wife could take care of her if only she wanted to. It's a strange thought but it makes a measure of sense to her—she wants to be part of a family.

And then she is pregnant.

Does she know she is pregnant, or does someone have to tell her?

Does she confide her symptoms to a girlfriend who says, You're pregnant!

Does she go to the doctor thinking she's ill?

Does she know that his wife is pregnant too?

She waits to tell him. The day he calls to tell her that his mother has died, she blurts, "We're going to have a baby." She wasn't exactly planning on doing it this way, but it just comes out.

She is thinking that it is good news, that it will make him happy, that now finally they will be together.

He is speechless.

His mother is dead, his wife is pregnant, and now she is too.

What was supposed to be a moment that would inexorably bond them—sharing the grief of his mother's death, sharing the news of a baby on the way—is all too much.

She is angry with him for not being pleased. He is angry with her for not being more careful.

They fight.

She is angry with herself and she is justifiably angry with the world. Is she angry with her baby?

He sends her to Florida, promising to follow. She waits

for him; he never shows up. When she moves back to Maryland they get an apartment together; he stays for four days before going home.

He offers to take her shopping to buy things for the baby.

His wife finds out that she is pregnant and lays down the law.

At some point she tells her mother, or maybe her mother just figures it out. Her mother looks at her and says, "You're pregnant, aren't you?"

She nods, wishing someone would have something nice to say. She likes being pregnant, likes the feel of this baby growing inside her, but has no idea what to do. She talks to her baby—she asks the baby, What should I do?

More pregnant and now unable to find work, she moves in with her mother, who has divorced the second husband.

In the end, in labor, she is alone at the hospital. And she still has the fantasy that he will come, that he will snap out of it and rush to her side. She wants to call him. A hundred times she wants to tell the nurse to dial his number.

"Where is your husband?" someone asks, and she cries hysterically.

The baby is beautiful. The nurses encourage her not to hold the baby. "After all, you'll never see her again," one of them says.

*   *   *

"You're making it up," someone says to me. Maybe and maybe not. I'm certainly imagining it. The only other option is for someone to tell me how it was, what really happened.

I think of Ellen and Norman before this, I picture them in the spring driving along the Potomac River in Washington, D.C., in a powder blue Cadillac convertible, the radio playing, wind blowing through their hair, and thinking, This is it, this is the life.

Claire Ballman

The Electronic Anthropologist

Jewel Rosenberg

I am compelled to look for more information—I have always known things that I don't know that I know. Unidentifiable bits and pieces would visit me in my mind's eye as if somewhere between dream and reality, but now I want to understand what I know and why.

The twenty-first-century search for roots is decidedly different from what it was as recently as the late 1990s. Now it is all about the Internet—Google, Ancestry.com, RootsWeb, and JewishGen. It is about electronic message boards and user-submitted family trees, and all of it a far cry from the days when you pulled out the family Bible and checked the names written in the front, when cousins lived next door, when you sat down and talked with old folks who, even if they weren't related, had known your family intimately for generations.

On the Internet, one can within seconds locate the long-lost and create a portrait of family out of the scraps of information that float randomly like atoms smashed, like fractured molecules desperate to reconnect. Every clue leads to another; first you find that there are several versions of the person you are looking for—the wrong ones, the almost right ones, and then *the* one.

Genealogical research is currently one of the top-ranked hobbies in the United States—in some ways it's more like a sport, collecting ancestors like baseball cards. It's also a kind of couch potato way of traveling through time—it's done in isolation, at odd hours, in a virtual world—and yet it is about connection, getting back in touch. And it is addictive. I am at it round the clock, a twenty-first-century Sherlock Holmes, trying to make this information age work for me. I pay $200 to join Ancestry.com. I buy electronic multipacks of articles from the *Washington Post* archive. I am perpetually punching in my credit card information—blindly buying anything that might be relevant.

*   *   *

I begin with my father's parents. I do not know their names, I know only that my mother told my father she was pregnant on the day his mother died—so I'm thinking it had to be sometime in 1961. I search the *Washington Post* archive and there she is, my grandmother Georgia Hecht—passed away on April 11, 1961. (Not so long ago, in my collection of stories *Things You Should Know*, I wrote about an unmarried woman getting pregnant. She names the child Georgica. Conscience, or coincidence?)

Each time I locate something—a detail, a fact, a missing fragment of information—I have the sense of having made a match. Something lights up. Bingo! We have a winner! And for a moment everything is clear, and then just as quickly I am all too aware that still, always and forever, there will be an enormous amount that remains a mystery.

My father's father is more difficult. Before I find him I locate his mother's parents. I put the name Georgia Hecht into a 1930 census search and find her living with my father, who is five, at her parents' house in Washington, D.C. Now not only do I have her maiden name—Slye—but I have her mother and father, my great-grandparents Mary Elizabeth Slye and Chapman Augustus Slye. I discover that Chapman A. Slye was a steamboat captain and also find in quick succession a dozen great-aunts and -uncles.

Within a week, I have traced the Slye family back to

George Slye, born in Lapworth, Warwick, England, in 1564. I locate Robert Slye, born July 8, 1627, in England, who came to America and in 1654 was named as one of the parliamentary commissioners to govern Maryland under Oliver Cromwell, lord high protector of England. He was also speaker of the Lower House of the Maryland General Assembly and captain of the colonial militia in St. Mary's County, and served as a St. Mary's County Court justice. Linda Reno, a wonderfully generous researcher I meet online, forwards a historical note showing that on April 24, 1649, a court in Hartford, Connecticut, fined Robert Slye ten pounds of tobacco for exchanging a gun with an Indian.

I am in the *Washington Post* archive looking up the Slyes, and there—buried in the January 25, 1955, obituary of Mary Elizabeth Slye, wife of the late Captain Chapman A. Slye, mother of "Mrs. Irving Hecht" (aka Georgia Slye)—is the information I've been looking for: Irving Hecht—my father's father. I try to find Irving Hecht in the census and can't—it is as though he was absent on the day in 1930 when they counted all the people. Who was he? Where was he? What were the circumstances that took him away from his wife and son? What did he do for a living?

Once it begins, the search is urgent; I am up in the night surfing, connecting the dots. Suddenly there are pieces of information I can't live without. Locating Irving Hecht takes me several more hours, but when I find his obituary—Thursday, July 5, 1956—I also find his brothers, Nathan of New York, Arthur S. of San Francisco, my great-uncles!

And as I am finding the right people I am also just as rapidly finding others that are right for a moment and then are proven wrong. For a long time I am sure one of the Harry Hechts is my grandfather, and then before I find the right Irving Hecht, I find the wrong Irving Hecht, living with his wife, Anna, and young son, Bertram, in Brooklyn on January 6, 1920. With each discard comes the lingering sense that invariably we're all interconnected, all responsible for one another, and that no one Hecht is any more or less compelling than the next. Coming from a position of having no history, having any history, even if it is the wrong history, is fascinating. Every life lived is of interest.

Bloodlines—I find myself more and more interested in the strangers I never knew, in the blood relations that are unveiling themselves before me. I notice that I am not as motivated to dig for the history of the mother and father I grew up with, and am not sure why. Is it because I already feel familiar and familial with them—or is there something psychically unique about discovering this new biological narrative? There is no escaping that what I am finding resonates; there is the hum of identification, a sense of wholeness and well-being. On a cellular level it makes sense—it matches. And simultaneously there is a kind of contradiction, a challenge to who I think I am, how I experience myself. The best way I can describe this experience, which eludes conventional language, is to say I think of this as the difference or dissonance between the unknown or dormant biological self that I arrived with and the adopted, adapted self that I became. The looking, the digging awakens numb spots, labyrinths in my own experience, in my ability to process. I feel a peculiar overexcited high and at other moments a devastating depression. I continue to dig, thinking that if I consume information, I will be able to inhabit it, I will feel more complete—not realizing that perhaps the exact opposite is just as possible.

The desire to know oneself and one's history is not always equal to the pain the new information causes. At times I have to slow down to accommodate a self that is constantly struggling to catch up, to recalibrate. I go to bed at midnight, and at 2 A.M. find myself at my desk—logging on. In the middle of the day I nap. My brain is constantly reshuffling the files and organizing and accommodating the new information. On the one hand I want to know my history, and on the other it is overwhelming to become aware of so many lives and to realize that most, if not all, of my ancestors are completely ignorant of my history and/or even my existence. There is a part of me that resents how hard I am working to locate information that they have lived with all along—information that is theirs for the asking.

I am looking at the records of the Slyes of St. Mary's County, who owned other people and who sold or gave them away. I am looking at these early settlers wondering, What were they thinking? Why, having come from such incredible privilege, did they not do more with their lives? They got here first, came with land and labor and power, and what did they end up building for themselves? Why did none become president, or direct a large corporation? Why did they not lay the railroad, or discover electricity? Why did they not start a nonprofit or fund philanthropy? I am frustrated with them for falling through the cracks of history. I think a lot about responsibility—did they take responsibility for who they were and what they did? What quality of people were they? And why does it mean so much to me? Why do I need for them to be good—better than good—need them to be great?

These are my souls.

I go to the New York City Municipal Archives at 31 Chambers Street. To get in, you have to show identification, tell them what you are there for, get a pass, and then go through metal detectors. I am stopped because somewhere in my bag I have a pair of tweezers. I leave the tweezers at the desk. In room 103, I sign in and pay $5 to use the microfilm machines. The people who work there have been there forever—they know the contents of each of the flat metal drawers, they know the Soundex system of organizing information, the difference between a marriage license and a marriage certificate. They know how to dig for buried treasure—but they are cranky about answering questions. It is like a civil servant episode of *Taxi*, with Danny DeVito playing the hostile clerk behind the counter.

Still, there is an undeniable beauty to the things found in this room—reels and reels of microfilm, images of lives lived long ago, documents writ in an ornate Old World hand of variable legibility. I go through the reels slowly at first, not wanting to fast-forward, not wanting to miss anyone, feeling like each one of them is due a visitor, an appreciation.

The room is full of people each piecing together their private puzzles and the first thing that occurs to me is they're not all adopted—so what are they looking for? I remind myself that the quest to answer the question *Who am I?* is not unique to the adoptee. In this room everyone is looking for something that will help them either confirm or deny part of what they believe about themselves. They are looking for backup, support, for definition. They are all deep in it—buried in names, dates, codes—but most are also happy to render assistance. Some volunteer helpful hints, while others tell their stories. I often ask, "How long have you been at it?" "Seven years," one woman tells me. "It started as a hobby, a birthday present for my husband," another says. "It started when my father died," another woman says. "Have you tried the Italians? They keep good records, even on the Jews."

Another woman leans over and whispers, "Have you been to Salt Lake City?" Salt Lake is "the mountain," the mecca for genealogical information—home base for the Mormons, who go around the world collecting genealogical data. Every month five to six thousand reels of microfilm are added to their collection. Unbeknownst to much of the general population, the reason the Mormon Church has such wonderful genealogical records is that they're collecting people—they hope to determine the genealogy of everyone in the world to prepare them for posthumous conversion. Basically they're making Mormons from the dead—baptism by proxy. They have a purification ritual through which they claim you as their own. There has been outrage from the Jewish community because the Mormons took the information of Holocaust victims— people who were killed because of their religion—and made them Mormons. In 1995 the LDS church said it would honor an agreement to stop the proxy baptisms of

Holocaust victims and other deceased Jews, and yet it continues. "And they are making more Mormons every day. I went once for two weeks," the woman tells me. "It was heaven. Think about it," she says.

There is the whir of the machines, juxtaposed against the virtual silence in which everyone works—it is difficult to stay focused. Repeatedly and anxiously I lose track of what I am looking for. A guy in a white shirt is hogging the files; he's got multiple drawers open, his arms filled with reels, and he's blocking the way. The rule is one reel at a time—take it, look at it, and put it back—which also makes it harder to misfile upon return. "Excuse me," I say, "it's one reel at a time." He ignores me. "Excuse me," I try again. "Just a minute," he grumps, digging through a drawer. I push my leg against the drawer, threatening to close it on his hand. "Excuse me—Is your dead person somehow more important than anyone else's?"

I find marriage certificates for David and Rika Hecht, my paternal great-grandparents, both born in Germany, and with each come the names of their parents, my great-great-grandparents: Nathan Hecht and Regina Grunbaum and Isaac Ehrenreich and Rosa Steigerwald. Within the hour I have birth certificates for Irving (born Isaac), Arthur Samson, and Nathan—my grandfather and great-uncles.

*   *   *

I locate Moriz Billman, born in Gomel, Russia, in 1846, who came into America in 1888 with a second wife and children from two marriages, and who later petitioned to become a citizen of the United States as Morris Bellman of 466 Bergen Street in Brooklyn. I find Billmans who became Bellmans and then Ballmans. I get a copy of the marriage license of my maternal grandfather, Bernard Bellman, to my maternal grandmother, Clara Kahn, and find that Bernard was married before and in 1925 divorced a woman named Margaret R. Bellman. Did his children—my mother and her brother—know? Were there other children from the first marriage? The man at the desk tells me that if I am curious I can look upstairs on the seventh floor—if the divorce was filed in New York City, I might just find it there.

With each name and date comes imagery. I start making mental pictures of who they were—who I might be. I am the granddaughter of an English Southern belle. I am the granddaughter of a Romanian/French immigrant. I am the granddaughter of the Lithuanian farmer girl, the granddaughter of the Russian bookie, the granddaughter of an Irishwoman. I am the adopted daughter of the guidance counselor and the left-wing artist and the biological daughter of the philandering adulterer and the wayward girl, the little girl lost.

*   *   *

I am back in time, wading across a clear running creek. I am a farmer on a plantation, I am captain of a ship. I am the woman in a long white dress, my curly hair high up on my head; I am feeling the heat of summer—the Southern humidity, the thick stagnant afternoon air, the coming of thunderstorms. I am conjuring sea captains and drinking glasses of blood red wine. This is the stuff of poems and fever dreams. I am of a plantation and I can say I knew it all along at some preconscious level. I am imagining the lives of indentured servants and slaves—some of whom had the very same names as the people I am looking for. When were they freed and where did they go?

What becomes clear is that all of this is about narrative—the story told. I can't escape the oddity of how it happened that I, a person without a past, became a novelist, a story-teller working from my imagination to create lives that never existed. Every family has a story that it tells itself—that it passes on to the children and grandchildren. The story grows over the years, mutates; some parts are sharpened, others dropped, and there is often debate about what really happened. But even with these different sides of the same story, there is still agreement that this is the family story. And in the absence of other narratives it becomes the flagpole that the family hangs its identity from.

As children we are all gullible by nature. It doesn't occur to us to question the family narrative; we accept it as fact, not recognizing that it is a story, a multilayered collaborative fiction. Think of the variations, the implications in terms of time, place, social status and structure. You are from Topeka and have been for five generations; your grandfather was a preacher, your grandmother half Indian. Or your grandmother is from a small village in Italy; she came here after her entire family was killed in a flood of volcanic ash when Mount Vesuvius erupted. Your mother was married once before and had a child she gave away— somewhere you have a sister. Your mother was out walking one night and someone came up behind her—and the product was you.

I take the elevator to the seventh floor. The smell of stale paper smacks you as soon as the elevator door opens; the hallways are filled with metal shelving units, packed with paper, precariously perched files that are threatening to tumble onto the floor. This is the history of New York, the history of America—and it's as though I've plunged into a Coen brothers movie.

It is a room of tables pushed together into a center square. There are current and not so current newspapers on the table and people sitting around, doing nothing—I am not sure if they work here or are people with nowhere to go. Maybe this is a historical day treatment center; maybe people are doing a certain kind of "time." The room is absent of air, of the passage of minutes, hours, and years. "Where would I find a divorce from the 1920s?" I ask the entire room. One man perks up. "Might be over here in the card catalog," he says, nodding toward the corner. There are huge metal cabinets, with cards for each lawsuit filed. Next to the card catalogs there is a large metal locker. Curious, I pry the door open. Old directories sigh and crumbling pages tumble out, dumping what looks like sawdust—or mouse bedding—onto the floor. Quickly I close the door and go back to the card catalogs. Again, I am flying blind, looking for anything and everything under any of the names on my list—Hecht, Bellman, Ballman, Billman.

"What kind of case is this?" I say, showing the man the card for *Hecht vs. in RE.*

"Oh, that's going to be interesting," the clerk tells me. Is he serious, or sarcastic? "The *in RE* cases usually mean that someone was either a minor or otherwise incompetent to represent themselves."

Just the phrase, "In Re:," gets my mind going. I sing to myself, "In Re:, a drop of golden sun."

"If you want the files you have to fill out a request—the old cases are stored off-site."

"Great, where's the form?"

"Sixty Chambers Street. Room 114."

*   *   *

Sixty Chambers Street is impossible to find, even though it's supposedly right around the corner. The narrow streets of lower Manhattan are dwarfed by large hulking buildings—some incredibly old, others more modern fortresses. Between the buildings there are police patrolling with machine guns in hand—this is our new world, post 9/11, and we seem to believe that people patrolling with guns makes us safer. There is a prison right there and a woman standing guard outside with a flak jacket and a big gun. "Excuse me, where is 60 Chambers Street?" She tells me, "I have no idea," and in a minute I discover that it is just across the street, and I'm thinking it's a problem that the guard doesn't know where she is and doesn't seem to care—especially if she had to tell someone where she was or which way someone went.

The dissonance is shocking—on the outside there is the Jersey wall, men and women with guns, the bright wash of summer light, the incredible baking heat, and inside, the smell of age, of mold and dust and things not touched for fifty years. I am depressed as hell, reminded of how unattached I am, and how crazy it is to do this digging—nobody cares. Whatever I find, it's only ephemera, the thinnest bits of information. I think of the papers that blew from lower Manhattan into Brooklyn when the World Trade towers fell, burned notes from people's desks, and how people clung to these scraps as if they held the secrets of the world, of creation.

At 60 Chambers the guard at the metal detector stops me and I confess that I have tweezers in my bag. He doesn't care. All he wants to know is, "Do you have a camera on your phone?" No. Inside I file my requests. It's noon. I am exhausted.

From my apartment I am exchanging e-mails with strangers and with relatives I have known for the whole of my life. I pull the adoptive relations in a little closer. I have the sense of belonging to my adoptive family more than I did as a child—this comes from having shared the experience of growing up within a narrative that, while it is not my own biologically, is now mine socially and culturally. I write to my adoptive maternal relatives in Paris and London. From them I collect tales of Jacob Spitzer's dairy farm on the Mohawk Trail in North Adams, Massachusetts— the dog, the cow, the horses, Nigger and Dick. There are stories about the children (the great-aunts and -uncles that I grew up with), Lena, Henry, Helen—who died in 1912 of diphtheria at fourteen—Maurice, Samuel, Solomon, (known as Charlie), Harold, Doris, and my beloved grandmother Julia Beatrice.

I collect information about Simon Rosenberg and Sophie Rothman—my adoptive maternal great-grandparents, born in the 1870s in Braila, Romania, a town on the Danube. My grandfather, Bernard, their eldest child, was born there in 1896, and by 1898 the family moved to an apartment at 64 rue Vieille du Temple in the Marais district of Paris. In France they had a successful hat factory and a very large family. My great-aunts and -uncles there include Rachel, who burned to death at three when the children were left home alone and her dress caught fire—my grandfather and his brother tried unsuccessfully to put the fire out. Among the other children were Joffre (who died at six), Raymond, Etienette, Henriette (who lived for six days), Adele, Maurice and Julien (who both died at Auschwitz), Emmanuel (who died of wounds in World War II), and another brother, Leon. In 1972, when my grandfather died in Washington, I got two of his hats, a winter hat and a summer hat. Elegant and understated, he never went out without a hat. At thirteen, I visited Paris and met Adele and Etienette. We went to 64 rue Vieille du Temple—my grandfather's family name was still on the buzzer, more than fifty years after the fact.

Through my adoptive father, several aunts in Florida, and a cousin ten blocks from me in New York, I cobble together the story of my adoptive paternal grandfather and grandmother—Jacob Homes and Minerva Katz. Throughout my childhood they never spoke of their past—I knew them only as hardworking people with a fondness for cheese Danish and stewed fruit. Jacob Homes (Homelsky) was born in Russia in 1892 and had three sisters and a brother. In 1910 he walked from Russia to Finland and found work on a boat, which landed him first in Canada and then in Philadelphia—where he earned enough to bring his mother and siblings to this country. In 1916 he met Manya Kvasnikaya (Minerva Katz) from Ekaterinoslav, Russia.

Minerva, the youngest daughter in a large family, was a late-in-life baby, rejected by her parents and largely raised by her oldest sister. She was educated for two years in a Russian school and then tutored by someone who gave her lessons while she sat atop a pickle barrel at the herring stall her sister ran. At home, Minerva slept above the oven on a bed of straw.

As a young teenager she traveled to the United States with her sister and brother-in-law, and they settled in northern New Jersey. She worked as a cashier in Atlantic City, went to school through sixth grade, and later lived in Philadelphia with a woman who sold goods to immigrants. There Minerva slept on a board over the bathtub.

In Philadelphia, Jacob Homes delivered meat from the butcher to the house where Minerva was living—he liked her because she could read and write. They married; a first son died at birth. In 1918 Joseph Meyer Homes, my adoptive father, was born, followed by five sisters. No one recalls whether Jacob's father came to this country—but all believe he was killed in an accident, run over by a wagon.

In 1929, when they were living in New Jersey, the

family's butcher shop burned down and they moved to Washington, D.C., where Minerva's brother lived. In Washington Jacob found a tank in a junk pile, filled it with gasoline, and took it to the farmers' market—selling gas by the five-gallon bucket to the farmers for their return trips after the market. He progressed to selling gas on the streets for ten cents a gallon and grew the business into the Homes Oil Company.

It was only when I started asking questions about the family history that my adoptive father told me one of the stranger stories of his youth—a moment where his own history collided with a particularly ugly and now forgotten moment in American history. In July 1932, he was working at his father's gas station on Maryland Avenue in Washington, D.C., when generals Douglas MacArthur and George S. Patton lead four troops of cavalry, four troops of infantry, a mounted machine gun squadron, and six tanks on a mission ordered by President Hoover to run the "Bonus Marchers" out of town. Soldiers on horseback with bayonets chased the Marchers—World War I veterans—out of their makeshift housing. Men and animals came charging right through the gas station. My grandfather grabbed my father and pulled him to safety. The story of my father and the Bonus Marchers—twenty thousand unemployed World War I veterans who marched on Washington, demanding payment of a cash bonus—is one that I hear for the first time when I am forty-four years old. I am thrilled to have it. I feel as though I'm slowly reconstructing an ancient lost tapestry.

At home in New York the electronic dig continues. I hire two researchers to help me—one in New York and one just outside Washington, D.C. We communicate by e-mail only. I tell them about the bits and pieces, the fragments of facts that I'm looking for, and they go in search. I am happy to have more than one mind on this—more than one thought pattern trying to piece the puzzle together.

I am in correspondence with someone living in Israel who may be related to my adopted father's family in New Brunswick, New Jersey. I am talking with the Reverend John Gray in Ohio, whose interest in genealogy was sparked by the idea that he might be related to his movie hero, Roy Rogers, aka Leonard Franklin Slye. The Reverend Gray sadly reports that he is not related to Roy, but in all likelihood I am—Roy was a Slye from Warwickshire, England, and Ohio. I am exchanging regular e-mails with Linda Reno in St. Mary's County, Maryland. She is, in fact, a distant relative and has done enormous research charting the Slye family. Each of my correspondents is as nearby as the computer keyboard, and yet as ethereal and vaporous as memory itself. And still and always I feel on the outside. I worry that at any minute I will be busted, and my pen pals will say, You are not part of this family, and you are not entitled to this information. With my chest tight I e-mail Linda Reno confessing my illegitimacy, and when I don't hear back for two days I am terrified—and then enormously relieved when I do, and her response is warm, genuine, and accepting.

It goes on for months—in waves. I hunt and gather and then, exhausted and often disheartened, I stop and I pull myself together and do it again. I become convinced that I can crack the case of my biological maternal grandmother's second husband—I have what I am quite sure is a photo of him and my grandmother, on what looks like a New Year's Eve in the 1950s. I find a lot of Barney Ackermans in Florida; it seems like the kind of place where a Barney Ackerman would retire. I find a scrap of information that seems to indicate there was a Barney Ackerman who died in Canada in the 1990s but I can't piece it together. When were Barney Ackerman and Clare Kahn Ballman married and divorced? Finally, through the Washington, D.C., researcher there is a crack in the case—she finds the wedding license. They were married September 22, 1950. Ellen would have been twelve years old at the time—vulnerable to this already twice-married stepfather. Another crack in the case brings me his obituary—it lists him as a dry cleaner and says that he was born in Calgary, Alberta, Canada, and died March 28,

1993, at the time of his death married to Jeanne Acker-man of Hebron, Nova Scotia. That makes at least four marriages—with the first divorce in Florida, the second in Reno, the third probably in northern Virginia around 1960. He has one daughter and at the time of his death one granddaughter. Did Ellen know he died—was she re-lieved? It was never clear to me what Ellen's relationship to this man was. From what she said to me in phone con-versations and from what Norman was later able to add, my sense is that the relationship was at least to a degree sexualized and made her very uncomfortable.

More digging. I find Pearl B. Klein, sister of Bernard Bell-man, admitted to the Washington, D.C., bar in 1924 at the same time as her husband, Alfred Klein, who later became chief law officer of the Civil Service Union.

I find Bernard Bellman's brother John (born Jake) Bellman, whose son Richard became a major figure in the mathematics world, conceiving the idea of "dynamic pro-gramming." Richard taught at Princeton and Stanford and worked for the Rand Corporation and at Los Alamos, while also writing forty books related to mathematical theory. I go back and forth through the material and each time I sift, new crumbs fall out—last names, the married names of sisters, the names of uncles, cousins, locations, each bit a piece of the puzzle.

My search expands. I use Internet search engines such

as AnyWho.com to locate addresses for random people named Slye, Bellman, Ballman, Hecht (there's almost no one named Homes). I write letters explaining that I am a journalist working on a family history project and would like to talk with them. As exciting as it is, I find it difficult to get the letters into the mail, difficult to make the follow-up calls. I want to talk to them, but I worry they won't want to talk to me—and by the way, what am I going to say if and when they ask me who I am?

I hire a graduate student to help me make the first round of calls, answering any basic questions—establishing that, yes, this is a legitimate research project. I do the follow-up interviews. I speak with two Slyes who happen to be reverends, Harry in Texas and John in Virginia—neither knows the other, but both are incredibly nice, warm, forthcoming, proud of their family. I talk with Chapman Slye, who runs twenty-eight school cafeterias in Fredericksburg, Virginia, and is named after my great-grandfather. Chapman tells me about the family ties to the Eastern Shore of Maryland, about the adventures he had with his grandfather Harry E. "Skipper" Slye Sr., a shipmaster who lived to be 102 years old and guided boats up the Potomac River until he was eighty-five. He also suggests I talk with his mother, widow of Harry E. Slye Jr. I speak with her and numerous other Slye cousins. And when I ask about Georgia Slye Hecht, no one seems to remember much, except that she was "formidable," "dominant," and many of them were a little scared of her—especially women marrying into the family. The Slyes I speak with are a lovely, hardworking, earnest, good-natured group, very proud of their family history; but as in many American families, each successive generation seems to move farther from the family seat and is less in touch with its extended family, less aware of the family history. They ask me nothing about how I might be related to the family and when I ask one of them if there was any intermarriage, he tells me that the biggest thing was when Catholics married into the family. There is no sense of there ever having been a Jew among them—no mention of Georgia Slye marrying Irving Hecht—which gives me further insight into my biological father, Norman's, determination to go out of his way to identify himself as *not* Jewish. The Reverend Harry L. Slye speaks of family reunions, long ago, when his grandfather, also Harry L. Slye, a prominent Washington, D.C., undertaker, would bring chairs from the funeral parlor out to the family home in the then rural suburbs, and the full extended family, cousins of all ages and generations, would gather, feasting on St. Mary's County oysters, playing games, and dancing on the lawn.

My assistant reaches someone in New York named Robert Hecht, who is not likely a relative. He tells her that he's leaving for Paris and I can call him there—I wait a few days and try. A woman answers the phone and explains that he's now gone back to New York. "What is this in reference to?" she asks and I am on the spot. I make an effort to explain. "I'm not sure he'll be interested," she says, "but you might want to e-mail my daughter and plead your case." She gives me the e-mail address of her daughter, a lawyer in New York. Ruffled by her use of the phrase "plead your case," I gather my courage and ask, "What's your name?" "Elizabeth Hecht," she says, and a chill runs through me. Elizabeth Hecht, that was my name—that was the name on the little bracelet that I wore home from the hospital. All the more odd because my adoptive mother had planned to name me Elizabeth but, when she saw the bracelet, she changed her mind. "Elizabeth Hecht," she says, and it was the last thing I was expecting. Chemicals of every sort flood my system, telling my brain to hang up, to flee, telling my brain to laugh, telling my brain this is so strange—she's not really Elizabeth Hecht; she was once Elizabeth Somebody Else and she married Hecht. "You can try my husband," she says. "He's back in New York."

I dial the number in New York; an older man answers and tells me this is not a good time for us to talk. "I'm on my way out."

The tenor of these conversations makes me wonder who these people are.

I Google Robert Hecht and Elizabeth Hecht and find out that he is a very famous dealer of antiquities and part of an international scandal involving the sale of allegedly stolen Italian artifacts, and as of the end of 2005 was on trial in Rome, along with former Getty Museum curator Marion True, accused of trafficking in ancient art.

As far as I can tell, Robert and Elizabeth Hecht are not my relatives, but again, I find the story fascinating.

One day as I'm going through the Bellman documents, I feel brave and leave a phone message for an Eric Bellman, a therapist in California. I call knowing that somewhere I have a relative named Eric Bellman—son of Richard Bellman and brother of Kristie, who I wrote to after Ellen died and never heard back from. It takes Eric weeks to call back, but it is a match. I'm pleased with my ability to deduce which of the Eric Bellmans in the United States is a biological relative. I tell him about my project, about the dozens of letters sent. I tell him that I've heard from a lot of Slyes and Hechts but no Bellmans. He tells me that Bellmans are like that—whatever "that" means— and while we don't have an enormous amount to discuss, I am glad to have made contact.

What I don't tell him is that after I decide that he was *the* Eric Bellman that I was looking for, I Googled his image and then compared the photograph I found online to one of his father taken many years ago. Playing my own version of FBI analyst, I compared their hairlines, their eyebrows, the shape of their chins and concluded that this Eric Bellman was the right Eric Bellman.

In my searching, I find newspaper clips relating to the Hecht family in and around the New York area. Again, I Google and come up with Warren Hecht, a dentist. I call his office. He answers the phone himself, I attempt to explain the project. "Write me a letter," he says gruffly. "Okay, but can I just ask you a quick question? Are you by any chance related to Arthur, Nathan, and Irving Hecht?" Elated, he repeats the names. "Arthur, Irving, Nathan," he says. "Yes, Nathan was my father." "I thought so." "Who is this?" He asks. We talk excitedly for a few minutes and he proposes that we meet the following Tuesday at 7 A.M. Surprised by his enthusiasm, I agree. It's as though he's discovered a long-lost relative—which in fact he has. When Warren asks how I fit in, I tell him that I am the daughter of Norman Hecht but that Norman and my mother weren't married, so I didn't grow up with him. That seems to land without much complication. He says how much he's looking forward to meeting me and we hang up.

The following Tuesday, my phone rings at six-fifteen in the morning. It's Warren Hecht calling to cancel our meeting. "I'm just too busy," he says. "I'll call you in a couple of weeks." When I push him to find out if he's really too busy, or if there's more to it, he seems nervous. I find myself wondering who got to him—who turned off the enthusiasm? Devastated, I let him go—I hadn't realized how much I was looking forward to meeting him. I

wanted to show him what I'd found, his father's birth certificate, his grandparents' marriage certificate. I wanted to
ask what he knew about his grandparents, his uncles, and
so on. After that, I decide to suspend the live interview
portion of the adventure at least for now. It's too much of a
setup for rejection and too painful to continually repeat.

I sign up for the National Geographic genealogy project. I
pay $100 and scrape the inside of my cheek, twice over a
period of twenty-four hours—collecting DNA—and send
it off, as if to join the family of man. Online I spot another
DNA test that promises to tell me the most likely names of
my ancestors. I think about how truly interesting and odd
it is that when a woman marries, traditionally she loses her
name, becoming absorbed by the husband's family name—
she is in effect lost, evaporated from all records under her
maiden name. I finally understand the anger behind
feminism—the idea that as a woman you are property to
be conveyed between your father and your husband, but
never an individual who exists independently. And on the
flip side, it is also one of the few ways one can legitimately
get lost—no one questions it.

Months later I go online, punch in the ID number that
came with my test kit, and am given the information that
my DNA belongs to the Haplogroup U, and that yes, like
every woman I am descended from "Mitochondrial Eve."

But who was she? Can I look her up on AnyWho.com? Can I write her a letter? From the information provided, I learn very little about my genetic journey. I am given the option of printing out high-resolution documents, including a personalized certificate that says I participated in the Genographic Project, but other than that I feel like I spent $100 to find out what I already know—I am related to everyone.

Among my best online discoveries is Random Acts of Genealogical Kindness, an organization of almost five thousand volunteers who will search for information in their local area—investigate historical records and church documents, trace headstones. Their volunteers are spread throughout the United States, Canada, and forty-four countries—the group averages eighty-two hundred requests a year.

Dipping further into history, I go to 60 Centre Street in New York City, another of the city's record offices, and request all files with the relevant surnames.

A week later the New York county clerk calls and leaves a message saying that some of my files have come in and that others cannot be located because they have been destroyed. Downtown I plunge into the labyrinth. Over a high wooden counter the case files are handed to me; they are crisp with age, these brittle documents, the onionskin paper dried out, each piece like a pathologist's slices of the skin. The pages are typed, the signatures and notations made with an inky black pen. I am pouring quarters into the Xerox machines, hurrying to photograph the faded pages—as though to copy them as quickly as possible before they evaporate, as though taking these poor copies out of the building with me makes them permanent, real, present in *this* world.

I examine the cases, having no idea if these people are related to me and to a large degree not caring. Each is a history, a story drawing me in.

```
Magdaline Bellman vs. William H. Bellman
```

```
Action for an absolute divorce alleging: "That
defendant on the 14 day of August 1923 at
Hollywood Crossing in Cedarhurst Long Island,
in the borough of Queens City and State of New
York committed adultery with a woman whose
name is unknown to the plaintiff. . . . That
the sole issue of said marriage is one child
Howard Bellman who was born on the 11th day of
February 1913.
```

The divorce, granted January 30, 1923, stipulates that William H. Bellman was not free to marry again without permission of the court. In January of 1934 William Bellman returns to court, asks for and receives permission to marry.

*   *   *

Did Magdaline Bellman really not know the name of the woman her husband slept with, or is this a way of being polite? Where at Hollywood Crossing did the affair occur—was it a motel? And is the street name Hollywood Crossing not incredibly ironic? Was the unnamed woman William slept with the same woman he married ten years later? What happened to Magdaline and her son, Howard? And are they related to me?

The clerk at 31 Chambers was right—the *in RE* cases are the most fascinating. The outer folders are stamped in faded large red letters: LUNACY.

```
        B. Kahn vs. In Re: Case 20101 1928
```

Bernhard Kahn of West 104th Street, born in Russia, aged fifty-four, arrived in the U.S., lived in Chicago and after being in New York six months, on May 19, 1928 was committed to Manhattan State Hospital, Wards Island.

He had been brought to Bellevue from the 10th precinct by ambulance.

```
Officer stated patient turned on fire hydrant on
Lexington Ave; said he wanted to wash down the
germs; the city was full of malaria germs and
insane germs and the people were all going in-
sane; had thrown away his hat because it was
full of germs and bugs——was talkative.
```

In the presence of the doctors, the patient said:

```
I went to Cook County hospital—they took so
many people from our trade and they tortured
and they killed them—In Chicago I was against
prohibition—I was against whores—We had had
brown taxis and yellow taxis—Three million
people tortured me in my city of Chicago—From
the psychopathic I came to New York—the Jews
are writing about the Hazenz here—then they
got the attendants who are insane—three de-
grees of insanity—there is no such thing as
perfect—I admire you—you are perfect.
```

Was there any one line in particular that sealed his fate?

When I first came across this case, I thought for a moment that this might in fact be the story of my biological mother's great-grandfather, and in that moment, it seemed to make sense. It still does in some way, except that the dates are way off. In my mind's eye it was a perfect case, until, of course, a more perfect fit came along—the case of Benedict Kahn.

```
BENEDICT KAHN, Plaintiff, against JACK ROTHSTONE
and JOHN J. GLYNN as administrators with the will
annexed of the Estate of ARNOLD ROTHSTEIN, de-
ceased, Defendants.
```

This case immediately reminds me of a line in Richard Bellman's autobiography, *Eye of the Hurricane*, noting that his father's brother Bernard "Bunny" Bellman "married the boss's daughter." For the first time I have a clue about what that might mean—I am thinking this case likely involves my mother's maternal grandfather, Benedict Kahn, and that it was through Benedict Kahn, that Bernard "Bunny" Bellman learned his trade.

Filed against the estate of the infamous gangster Arnold Rothstein, who was shot on November 4, 1928, the case states that Benedict Kahn and his business associate Harry Langer—who filed a separate case for $76,000—both made loans to Arnold Rothstein that had not been paid back at the time of his death. Benedict Kahn's affidavit reads:

```
I am the plaintiff herein. This action is
brought to recover $21,000 with interest
thereon upon two promissory notes aggregating
$19,000 and a check of $2000.
```

It goes on.

```
I never gambled with Arnold Rothstein in my life
time. I never borrowed any money from him. He
and I were intimate personal friends, and from
time to time he borrowed money from me. He knew
I was always possessed of large amounts of cash.
```

Nowhere in the papers is there any explanation of what business Kahn was in that had him "always possessed of large amounts of cash." Basically there was no defense for this case because the only option was for the Rothstein estate to prove that this was a gambling debt and therefore not legal or valid.

After much back-and-forth the motion for a judgment is granted, "in favor of the plaintiff for $21,000, together with interest, as demanded in the complaint."

The fact that the man who appears to be Ellen's maternal grandfather had the nerve to make a case against the estate of Rothstein, a man described as "the spiritual father of American organized crime," and a "criminal genius," tells me that Benedict Kahn must have been someone that both the estate and the court took seriously—but beyond that I find nothing, except the seeds of a strong interest in numbers and gambling that echoed throughout subsequent generations.

And then there is the sad story of the Bellman who got bumped on his head—big time. Here is another Henry— this time Bellman, not Hecht—but for inexplicable reasons, I remain convinced that somewhere I do have a biological relative named Henry.

> Henry Bellman vs. In Re: George Bellman vs.
> Timken Silent Automatic Co.

Henry Bellman, born in Germany in 1902, arriving in New York in 1928, is brought to Bellevue saying he can't sleep, has a headache, lights are bothering him. In the presence of the doctors, he said:

```
The way it looks they throw lights, right into
my room, and I can't sleep. I hear them talk-
ing. They laugh at me. I moved five times in
three or four months. They follow me in the
street. They make fun of me. I heard them say
c.s. and s.o.b. I don't know if they want to
kill me. They are down here too.
```

He was committed to Central Islip State Hospital.

George Bellman as guardian for Henry Bellman files a case against the Timken Silent Automatic Co. asking for $150,000 in damages, stating that Henry, never injured or ill, working as a driller for $8.80 a day, was on September 8, 1934, on First Avenue between Ninety-sixth and Ninety-seventh Streets, struck by a truck. The truck, which swerved to avoid a granite block in the roadway, bumped another car into a ditch, and then ran through a barricade, striking Henry Bellman, knocking him unconscious for more than ten minutes. His injuries, initially thought to be mild, became progressive. His condition deteriorated, and in July 1935 Henry began to complain that people were spying on him. The case was filed first by Henry and then by the family—seeking to be able to afford a better-quality care for their brother. It was settled without trial for $27,500, of which $13,750 was paid to the attorney the brother hired before his condition had so deteriorated. The Honorable Edward R. Koch was presiding justice, April 8, 1936. Case file stamped LUNACY.

I can't help but think about the difficulty of these immigrants' lives, of Bernhard Kahn and Henry Bellman and thousands of others. They left their homes and families in Europe under what were often pressured and fearful circumstances. With only the belongings they could carry on their backs they set off on a difficult journey to a mythical faraway place, hoping for Utopia, finding instead a foreign language, discrimination, and poor working and living conditions. I am amazed at the resilience and fortitude most immigrants demonstrated and am also surprised that more didn't simply go mad—there are times I think, how could you not?

Whether or not Magdaline, William, and their son, Howard, or Bernhard or Henry are related to me by blood, they are all related by humanity and by the stories the files tell, and it is all lunacy! I am including the stories here because I cannot bear for them to be forgotten.

I continue to dig, off and on, stop and start, and collect the fragments of hundreds of lives. The technicality of biological relation becomes somewhat irrelevant—I am thrilled by what I am finding, by dipping into history, by seeing how people lived and died, noticing what else was going on in the world at each of these points. As stressful it has been, I have enjoyed the process; it amazes me how deep and expansive the World Wide Web is (at only fifteen years old) and I am thrilled to have met and corresponded with so many people along the way. My search is no longer all-consuming, the initial urgency has settled into a perhaps healthier continuing curiosity and no doubt will continue on and off over time. And yes, there is comfort in having connected some of the dots—in having names and dates and some sense of where my family lines and I fit into history. I can juxtapose Robert Slye's birth in England with the reign of Queen Elizabeth. I note that Friedrich Nietzsche is born in the same year as Jacob Spitzer (the father of my beloved grandmother Julia Beatrice), and that in 1959, the year of my brother Jon's birth, the Dalai Lama escapes Tibet and goes to India, while Alaska and Hawaii become the latest additions to the United States. In January 1961, the year of my birth, at the inauguration of John F. Kennedy, the American poet Robert Frost stands to recite a new poem, "Kitty Hawk," but is frail and fumbles the words. He begins again, instead reciting "The Gift Outright."

Norman Hecht as a boy

My Father's Ass

Norman Hecht as a young man

have not spoken to my father since the conversation in late 1998 that ended with him saying I could call him anytime—"Call me in the car, my wife's not usually in the car."

In the summer of 2005, as an extension of my genealogical adventure, I decide to join the Daughters of the American Revolution. My desire is not political but personal. I want to join the DAR because it is a lineage organization—and among the first things my father told me about myself was that I am eligible. And while I am an unlikely member of such an organization, I want to try it on as a piece of my biological identity—I want to see from the inside the thing that I am not. My friends are upset by the idea; they view the DAR as right wing and racist. In 1939 the DAR refused to allow the black singer Marian Anderson to sing at Washington D.C.'s Constitution Hall. (Subsequently Miss Anderson sang at Constitution Hall six times.) I explain to my friends that understanding my background is not just about embracing the parts that feel comfortable, and that, in this case, my interest is in the concept of lineage. I trade e-mails with the president of the Port Tobacco, Maryland, chapter—the hometown chapter of the Slyes of Maryland. She sends me a copy of the worksheet, which asks the applicant to walk back through time and provide the documentation for fourteen generations proving the link to the one deemed "the Patriot."

I am assured that this documentation can be assembled if I can provide the more current information—namely my father's birth certificate and my own. A complication—my father's name is not on my birth certificate. And my father's birth certificate is available from the District of Columbia Department of Vital Records, but only to next of kin—photo ID required. I explain to the DAR that my birth parents were not married and that I was adopted and I do not have a birth certificate with my father's name on it, but that my father and I had a DNA test to prove our relationship. The DAR responds that they do not care if my parents were married or not, they will accept the DNA test as sufficient proof. A further complication—I don't have a copy of the results.

Why didn't I ask him for a copy of the test in July 1993 when the blood was drawn? I could say I felt shy, but the truth is I felt infantile—thrown back through time. It was all I could do to hold on to any semblance of self. I wanted him to like me, I wanted to know more about who I was, where I had come from. I felt I had to do what I was told. As much as he and I were equal participants in the test, he paid for it, refusing to accept my offer to share the expense. I was intimidated. I didn't want to cause trouble. I didn't want to be rejected again.

I imagine asking him and am intimidated even now. Just the idea of it hurts. And I always worry that my call will come too late—he will be dead. And even if he's not, what will I say—"Hi, I want to join the DAR and I need a copy of your birth certificate and the DNA test?"

I imagine him answering the phone—his voice will tremble and he'll say, "This is not a good time—can I call you back later?" How will I feel if he doesn't call back? And what if I do manage to ask for what I want and he stalls, and there is an awkward and heavy silence? Do I continue, "We were equals in submitting to the test and both have the right to the information?" And if he says, "I don't think so," I'm not sure where I go. "I've never asked you for anything, but now I am asking you for something and I hope you will reconsider."

I think of calling him—in my imagination, his wife answers the phone, and is not pleased. To her I am illegitimate. Does it mean I don't exist, that I never existed, that I am something to be forgotten, left behind, basically a big embarrassment?

In my thoughts I can call him; in reality I can't pick up the phone.

I ask Marc, my lawyer—the same lawyer who called him years ago to tell him Ellen was dead—if he would mind giving him a call. I give Marc the phone number and explain that his wife might answer. We discuss what he is going to say. The call is made.

The wife answers the phone and my father goes into another room to take the call. My father tells my lawyer that he will not provide the test result, that in fact he does not even have the test result—he gave it to his own lawyer for safekeeping. Marc is told that he should not call my father anymore, that any further communication should go through my father's lawyer. Marc calls my father's lawyer and the lawyer tells him that, yes, he did have the test result but that he did something with it—can't remember what, so it's not to be had. Marc tells him that an affidavit of paternity will do and is told that that's not possible, that's not going to happen.

Call me naive—there was part of me that thought when my lawyer called and asked for the test results, the answer would be, Yes, of course, and how is she?

When Marc calls to tell me how it went I'm feeling hopeful, cheered by the swiftness of the response. "I spoke to your father," he says and I'm pleased, proud in a certain way, and then he says, "And it didn't go well," and my spirits sink. "He declined to provide the information and asked that we not contact him directly again." That's my father we're talking about—my father is saying, Please don't call again. Was it something I said, or just the fact of my existence?

The idea that my father asked me to participate in a DNA test—asked me to prove myself to him—and now won't share the results is not okay. It is about power and arrogance and the negation of my right to own my identity. I feel a moral obligation—a social and political obligation, an obligation that is larger than me—to try and get a better resolution, a better end.

"What did you expect?" a friend asks.

"More," I say.

"This is nothing new," she says. "He's behaving in character. Look at what he did to your mother. He's not a good guy."

"He's my father."

"You're screwed."

I am waiting for this man to do the right thing. What I want from him is not his money or even his love—at this point, in the absence of his affection, I want a context, a history, a way of understanding how all this came to be.

Will I ever have the question answered: Where did my paternal grandparents meet, what was their courtship like, how did it happen that the son of a Jewish butcher married a Southern belle?

And now I also have to defend my dead mother. My friend is right about this. It's not about me, it's about him, it's about the way he behaves, how he values people, how he does only what he wants, what's good for him. My mother had no life after she gave me up—she never married, never had another family. She had invested in him from a very early age—he used her and then said goodbye. She never recovered.

"Law is not about what is fair, you realize that," a friend says to me.

I call another friend, who calls Lanny Davis, a well-known Maryland lawyer who acted as special counsel to the White House under Bill Clinton. I remember Davis from when I was growing up and he was an up-and-coming local politico. I instinctively trust him and explain the situation. Lanny offers to make a call for me; he is quite sure that if he explains the situation to my father—and the reason that I am asking for this document—it will be forthcoming.

"There's no reason to think we'll have to take this further." I give him the telephone number and again mention that the wife might answer the phone. He calls me the next afternoon—shocked. My father took his call, seemed to know why he was calling before he even said anything, and flat out refused. Lanny, being careful about his description of the events, told him, "I was approached by your daughter and asked to consider representing her, but having heard the story, it is my hope that this can be resolved without my having to put my lawyer hat on." Norman refused. "Should I put my lawyer hat on? Should I be speaking with your lawyer?" My father refused to even tell Lanny his lawyer's name and/or provide the lawyer's phone number—both of which I already had.

Lanny called my father's lawyer. The lawyer said, "You don't have a leg to stand on, there is nothing to go to court about, there is no case, and you cannot have the document." He said no and no and no. The lawyer was cautiously reminded that if this became a court case it also became a public event. He was unfazed.

"Is there anything else I should know?" Lanny asked me. "Some other reason why he wouldn't want you to have this?"

"There are only two things I can think of: one is that he is not really my father, but somehow wanted to be, in some strange way; or maybe he's worried I'll make a claim on his estate."

Long ago, when he stopped talking with me, I thought it might be because he was worried that I would sue his estate for a "piece of the pie." I explain to Lanny I want nothing from his estate and in fact would feel compelled to refuse anything were it to come.

Once again in my head I am writing letters.

Dear Norman,

Are you kidding? You are writing your own history. You are painting a portrait of yourself that is less than flattering—want to reconsider?

I confer with lawyers—everyone is surprised. It shouldn't be this difficult.

"Is it something about your family and the DAR? Something maybe you don't know? Something that bubbles beneath?" someone asks.

What bubbles beneath is rage—nuclear-hot rage. And below that, deep grief—profound disappointment that he is not capable of more, cannot rise to the occasion, does not feel compelled to do better.

I go to see the rabbi. I am hoping for some insight, hoping there is learned example, spiritual intervention that will guide my decisions. We talk a lot about what is to be gained and what is to be lost—the actual importance of the piece of paper and the larger picture.

The rabbi suggests I write a letter—a simple note: I am writing to let you know that if I don't hear from you to the contrary, I am going, from now forward, to act as if and assume that you are my biological father.

The rabbi suggests that I run that past the lawyer. I do and the lawyer points out that it proves nothing, that it simply sets me up to wait—for nothing.

I write more letters in my head:

Dear Dad,

My interest in the DAR is about genealogy and lineage and I cannot let your actions stop me from joining with hundreds of years of my biological decedents.

You long ago promised to take me into your family—and I understand that life and families are complicated things. What I am asking for is not about your immediate family, your sons and daughters who are biologically no more or less related to you than I—what I am asking you for is to provide the link, so that I may make my own connection to my past, allowing me to join my relatives of the last four hundred years. It is the history that interests me, the history of all of the families that I am part of. . . .

Dad—

You fancy yourself a man of belief, of good character; I would think as one grows older one would think about that belief, about what one's God expects of him, about one's behavior through the course of his lifetime. I am a person of great optimism and faith and it remains my hope that we can resolve this with some measure of grace.

Pop—
Take responsibility for your actions, be a bigger person, be a man.

Mr.
You are an old man——don't you want peace, don't you want people to feel good about you?

Dad—
Fine thing. Isn't that your expression for events such as these?

The lawyers debate what to do—is there a way to compel him to produce the document? If we were to take him to court, what would we take him to court for—breach of contract? unfair use of the results? He's had more than 50 percent use of a co-owned result for all these years. If in fact he lied to me, saying, I want you to do this test so I can take you into my family, when he may have wanted the results to explicitly exclude me from his family, from his estate—it's fraud. Was he acting fraudulently?

"Where was the test done?" one of the lawyers asks me.

"The blood was drawn in Washington, D.C."

"What was the name of the lab?"

"I don't remember. I'm not sure it even had a name—it wasn't so much a lab as an office, a collection site."

"Maybe you can get the result directly from the lab."

Once again I am digging. I am looking for blood labs that did DNA blood testing in 1993—before it was all the rage, before everyone and their mother wanted to know who throughout history was their brother. I uncover Orchid Cellmark—the leader in DNA testing—and give them a call.

"This is Jennifer," the voice of Orchid Cellmark says.

"Hi, I'm trying to locate the results of a DNA blood test I had done in 1993."

When I say 1993, it's as though I'm saying 1903—the world we are living in is so brutally advanced and ahistorical.

In a millisecond Jennifer tells me, "Oh, we wouldn't have that. Anything over five years we don't keep."

"What do you do with it?"

"We shred it," Jennifer says. And I don't believe her. I'm thinking, Jennifer, you can't shred it because it doesn't exist on paper—it lives in a computer. And then images of laptop computers being fed into a giant shredder fill my mind.

"Thanks," I say, hanging up. I try another lab.

According to Pat at LabCorp of America they too don't have the results. "We keep our records for seven years."

"When did you start doing DNA testing?"

"Hold on."

I'm on hold with tin can music in my ear. I'm on hold for a long time and it occurs to me that she just put me on hold to make me wait and is sitting there on the other end, picking her nose. It occurs to me that she might not come back. "First in its industry to embrace genomic testing," says the background tape.

"Nineteen eighty-one," she says, coming back on the line. There is a peculiar coldness, a kind of self-satisfaction to the way these people say, We don't have that, as though they have no idea what that might mean, they really don't care, as though they get enormous and perverse pleasure from emptying the electronic trash can on their computer screen. Gone, gone, and gone.

One of the lawyers asks if I have any letters from him. I think somewhere I might have a birthday card. Would there be enough DNA on the envelope to get a result? And anyway, without him already in a database, how would we deny or confirm?

Again the lawyers debate. We talk about the fact that I have not said his name in public, have never printed the information. I am wondering if my father realizes that until now I've never told anyone who he is. In fact, the origin of this book, a long piece I wrote for the *New Yorker* in 2004, reflected my desire to continue to protect him. In that article, I called Norman "Stan" and Ellen "Helene." I'm wondering if Norman knows that what I wrote for the *New Yorker* was so convincing that when it was time for the magazine to fact-check the article, they e-mailed me and asked for "Stan's" phone number. "My father's name is not really Stan," I explained. And again they asked for his name and number. I told them that I had never given anyone that information and I would not be able to provide it to them.

Only after the magazine first threatened and then did briefly kill the piece did I question why I was ruining my professional reputation protecting the identity of someone who had never shown any particular concern for me. Still, I didn't think they needed to bother the man. They insisted. The *New Yorker* has what they call a double standard for fact checking—if the subject is to be unidentified or masked, not only does the subject have to be rendered unrecognizable to others, but also unrecognizable to himself. My father, simply by knowing that he is my father, had his cover blown.

The way the magazine killed the piece—as if doubting me—practically killed me. For the first time in years, I felt that my right to exist was in question. That there was any doubt to the truth of my story sent me into a spin. It had never been my desire to expose my father—and at the same time I couldn't help but wonder, why was I being so protective? Finally I gave the *New Yorker* his phone number. I have no idea what was said between the magazine and my father and his lawyer. I asked to be there, a witness to the conversation, but the fact-checker refused. From what the fact-checker told me, I understood there were thirty-five questions the magazine wanted to ask; they detailed them for my father and his lawyer—and my father and his lawyer declined to answer any of them. The piece was published by the *New Yorker* in December of 2004.

I confer with my lawyers about the DAR application—it occurs to more than one of them that the lawyer for my adoptive parents might actually have a copy of my original birth certificate, because it was a private adoption and because my mother never signed the papers, and *someone* had to provide the court with a copy of the original birth certificate.

The lawyer I have to call is the man who called my parents in 1992 to tell them that Ellen had contacted him, the same lawyer who opened the letters from Ellen, who recognized my father's name and called Ellen to say, if you're going to give *her* (me) that information, you'd better tell *him*.

Dialing the lawyer's house, I have chest pains. His wife answers—she is tentative when I ask for him. "May I ask who's calling?"

"A.M. Homes."

"May I ask, what is it about?"

And I explain, "Mr. Frosh helped my parents finalize my adoption back in 1961. It was a private adoption and I spoke with him several years ago when my birth mother contacted him trying to reach me—and now I have some questions."

There is a pause. "He's not entirely well."

"I'm so sorry," I say, wondering what that means—again, always the fear that I've called too late.

"He's eighty-seven and some days he knows everything and the next remembers nothing. But I will ask him when it seems like a good moment."

"Thank you," I say. "What I'm looking for is the file, a copy of the file."

"Maybe my son Brian," she says.

"Yes," I say, "if he could find it, that would be great. I think he knows about it. When my birth mother called, she actually first called Brian." (Brian is also a lawyer).

And then she tells me a story of someone, maybe her daughter, maybe a neighbor, having adopted two Romanian children. At this point I'm having what I call situational deafness. I am worrying about the fact that I may not be able to get this information. I've half of a mind to say: Do you know where he kept his files? Are they stored somewhere? But instead I say, "Did it work out?" And I think she says yes, and I say something like,

"That's good. Good or bad, up or down, it's all interesting, isn't it?"

"Are you having a good life?" she asks, like she wants to know, did it all work out?

"A good life? Yes," I say, both lying and not. I'm having a great life. "I'm really lucky. I have a great life." And it is equally true that I am suffering, otherwise I wouldn't be calling her. "Everything is good," I tell her.

"That's good," she says. "Have a good life."

I contact the lawyer's son Brian Frosh, now a Maryland state senator. We exchange e-mails; I tell him about my conversation with his mother and remind him of the call he intercepted from Ellen years ago. I ask Brian if, when he visits his parents' house, he might check for the file. He is incredibly gracious and understanding. We trade stories of what it is like to have an aging parent, our concerns for our families, for the history that is lost. Brian Frosh makes a special trip to his parents' house to look for the file—he looks everywhere, but finds nothing.

I am running out of options.

The question of whether or not to sue, to attempt to legally compel my father to produce the DNA document or an affidavit, remains open. Joining the DAR is not essential to my health and well-being, but the idea that my father—or any one person—can decide to exclude someone from her lineage profoundly bothers me. The real question is not about the DAR but about adoptees' rights to access and join their own heritage—and for that reason I am not entirely willing to drop the subject.

I think of my father asking me to have the DNA test and then later refusing my request for the DNA document, refusing to sign an affidavit, and refusing to acknowledge me. I think of my father and can't help but think of Ellen—falling for him when she was just a teenager, being his mistress for seven years, and then pregnant with his child. I think of Ellen and I think of how my father behaved—making her promises, stringing her along, and ultimately abandoning her.

Nothing has changed. More than forty years later he is still behaving exactly as he always behaved. He is doing what is good for him, what suits his needs and desires. I see my mother as a teenager in love with an older man, a young woman who had to give up her child, who lived the rest of her life in the shadow of that loss, a woman who never married, who never really recovered—and for her I am angry with him.

This is not just about the DAR—that's clear. I wish there had been more: a father-daughter relationship, a friendship. I wish I could know more about his family (my family)—where they came from, how they lived their lives, what they valued. I would have liked to know his children, to learn what we have in common, to feel what it means to have a blood knot. And I would have liked to have come out from the shadows, to be seen not as the product of an affair but as a person, an adult—who is no more or less *of* them than they are *of* one another.

Based on nothing except my own blind faith, I am cautiously optimistic that there will be some natural opening, some give on Norman's part. I resolve to do nothing for the moment, to watch and wait, to allow myself to catch up to my feelings and to see over time where the story leads me.

Like an Episode of *L.A. Law*

Deposition: a curious word meaning to remove from office or a position of power and/or testimony under oath—a written statement by a witness for use in court in his absence.

Deposition: I think of suing my father to prove that he is my father and just the phrasing—suing my father to prove that he is my father—has the equally surreal echo of the moment my mother told me that my mother was dead. Suing my father—I picture the papers being filed, a summons served telling him to appear at a certain place at a certain time. I imagine there being a man, a stranger to both of us, someone hired to do the job, to ask the questions.

Mr. Hecht, before we begin I would like to remind you that the length of a deposition is limited to seven hours a day, over the course of however many days it takes to do the kind of call-and-response, asking of questions, related to the actions and activities of the last forty-four years—that's how old she is now, the infant in question.

Rules of Civil Procedure. Rule 26—Discovery. We will be asking you, the deposed, to provide a copy of your birth certificate and a copy of the DNA test that you and Ms. Homes jointly participated in. Given that a potential witness is anyone who has information relevant to the issues of a lawsuit or who has information that may lead to relevant information, we will also call your wife and your children. Unlike a trial, where a judge can rule on objections, at a deposition lawyers can ask irrelevant questions and inquire into hearsay.

Is all of this clear?

Have you ever had your deposition taken before?

Do you understand that you are under oath—sworn to tell the truth?

Are you prepared to answer my questions?

Is there anything about your physical state—are you taking any medications that will prevent you from giving me complete and truthful answers?

If you need to take a break at any time, let me know.

What is your full name?

Your place and date of birth?

Your parents' names and places and dates of birth?

Mr. Hecht, can you tell me why are we here today? Is there a particular issue?

In 1993 you asked Ms. Homes to participate in a DNA blood test that would genetically compare DNA samples from both you and Ms. Homes to prove that in fact you are her father. And the result of that test showed that it was 99.9 percent likely that you are her father, and recently when she requested a copy of that test from you, you declined to provide it—is that correct?

You asked Ms. Homes to participate in the test, but you don't believe you should both have access to the results. Why is that?

You participated equally?

You paid for the test, Mr. Hecht—actually you had some trouble paying for the test, didn't you? You scheduled the appointment for the test in July of 1993, Ms.

Homes traveled from New York to Washington and met you at the lab, but you didn't have the right kind of payment, the right kind of check—and you had to go back again the next day?

At the time you scheduled the test, Ms. Homes offered to pay for the test as well or split the cost with you?

Now, if it is all about the money—the costs associated with this meeting here today are in excess of the charges for the test. So perhaps this is not about money?

How would you describe yourself, Mr. Hecht?

Would you describe yourself as a family man?

Is there more to you than that—than just a retired businessman?

Are you close to your family?

Do you go to church?

You have a son who shares your name—what does that name mean to you?

What is your identity, Mr. Hecht?

Did you always know who you were?

Have you ever been arrested?

Been charged with a crime?

For the record, can you tell us about any and all claims, lawsuits, that you've been involved in over the years?

What was your age and place of first employment?

And your last—were you fired, or asked to step down?

Did you feel any personal responsibility?

Do you think of yourself as someone who gets things done?

Has anyone ever called you a big shot?

Do you think you're an average man?

Same level of ambition as your peers?

Did you graduate from college?

Were you in the army? Ever kill anyone?

Where did you grow up, Mr. Hecht?

How would you describe your childhood?

Who raised you?

How was it that you lived with your grandparents—where were your mother and father?

How did your parents meet?

What did your father do for a living?

How would you describe your relationship with your father?

Were you close?

Did he love you?

Do you think it's true that boys are closer to their mothers, and girls to their fathers?

Are you proud of your family history?

Involved in any lineage organizations?

What clubs are you a member of?

Have you ever wanted to join a club and not been allowed in?

What kind of name is "Hecht"?
Was your father Jewish?
Was he raised in a Jewish home?
Did your mother's family consider you Jewish?
Was your father's father a kosher butcher?
Why did your paternal grandmother carry a gun?

Would you describe yourself as charitable?
Do you give money to charities?
Do you give of your time and abilities?
Do you drink?
Did you ever use recreational drugs?
Ever smoke marijuana?
Ever take pills for energy?
Ever use cocaine?
Ever try Viagra?

Where did you meet your wife?
At what age were you married?
Did you engage in relations before the wedding?
Was she a virgin?
Were *you*?
Have you ever had a sexually transmitted disease?

When did you last have sex, Mr. Hecht?
With whom?

Would you say that you and your wife had a good sex life?

Did you and your wife ever discuss open marriage?

So, initially she didn't know that you were having a sexual relationship with Ms. Ballman?

Was Ms. Ballman your first relationship outside your marriage, or did someone precede her?

How did your wife find out about Ms. Ballman?

Can you tell me the names of your children?

Do you know their birth dates?

Besides Ms. Homes—did you have any other children outside your marriage?

Is it possible, Mr. Hecht, that there are others?

How many relationships did you have outside your marriage?

How long did they last?

Your wife was pregnant at the same time as Ms. Ballman?

How old was Ms. Ballman when you met her?

How would you describe her physically—her appearance?

Did you know that she was a minor?

What were the circumstances of that meeting?

Were you the owner of the Princess Shop?

How long did Ms. Ballman work for you?

When did your sexual relationship begin?

What were the circumstances of that first encounter?

Was she a virgin?

Do you think your libido is average?

Was Ms. Ballman a nymphomaniac?

Was she a lesbian?

Did you once tell Ms. Homes that Ellen Ballman was a nymphomaniac and on another occasion that she was a lesbian?

Did your male friends also have girls on the side?

How many of them knew Ms. Ballman?

Did you worry that Ms. Ballman was sleeping with other men—your friends?

When your sexual relationship with Ms. Ballman began, how old was she?

What would prompt a teenage girl in the 1950s to leave her mother's care and take up with a married man?

Did Ellen Ballman tell you that someone was molesting her?

You told Ms. Homes that Ms. Ballman told you something that would have indicated that something was happening in her mother's home and that you probably should have listened better.

Did you take advantage of Ms. Ballman?

Did you use birth control?

*   *   *

Did Ms. Ballman meet your family—your mother?

Your children?

Your wife?

How did it happen that your eldest son spent time with Ms. Ballman?

When did you realize you were in love with Ms. Ballman?

So, were you or were you not in love with Ms. Ballman?

Did she believe you were in love with her?

On more than one occasion did you propose marriage?

Even though you were already married, Mr. Hecht, you proposed to Ms. Ballman when she was seventeen— you called her mother and asked for permission to marry her?

How did you think you would explain that to your wife?

Do you believe in polygamy, Mr. Hecht?

How and when did your wife find out that you and Ms. Ballman were having a relationship?

Did your wife know how old Ms. Ballman was?

And what did you say to your wife? Again I'd like to remind you that you are under oath and your wife will be answering the same question.

Did your wife contemplate divorcing you?

Is divorce in opposition to her faith?

Are you and your wife of the same faith?
Is adultery in opposition to your faith?
Are you a religious man, Mr. Hecht?
Do you believe in heaven, Mr. Hecht?

What was your nickname for Ms. Ballman?
Was "the Dragon Lady" one of them?
Where did that come from? Was it from something you shared?
Did Ms. Ballman have you arrested for deserting her?
When Ms. Ballman was pregnant, you sent her to Florida to live and said you'd be joining her there—but you never showed up?
And your wife was pregnant at the same time as Ms. Ballman?
You must have felt like an exceptionally fertile man?

Later in the pregnancy did you visit Ms. Ballman at her mother's home?
Did you offer to take her shopping and buy things for the baby?
Did you have Ms. Ballman meet with you and your lawyer and together discuss the fact that "there are only so many slices of the pie"?
Did you ask either Ms. Ballman or your wife to consider an abortion?
Can you swim, Mr. Hecht?

I'm just wondering if at some point during all this you felt like you were going under. Drowning.

When was the last time you saw Ms. Ballman pregnant? What month was that?

How did you hear about the birth of your child with Ms. Ballman?

Were you ever asked to sign any legal documents relating to the child?

How long did your relationship with Ms. Ballman last?

Did Ms. Ballman ever marry?

Are you proud of your daughter, Mr. Hecht?

Are you proud of Ms. Homes?

Have you read her work?

Did you ask your daughter to meet you in hotels?

Why not coffee shops?

What is the nature of your thoughts about your daughter?

Did your wife know when and where you were meeting your daughter?

If you had been meeting one of your other children, would she have known?

Are you circumcised?

Is this common knowledge?

Does your other daughter know?

Why was this information that you shared with Ms. Homes?

How did your other children find out that they had a sister?

And what was their reaction to discovering that information?

Do you think of yourself as a good father?

Let's backtrack a little bit . . .

In May of 1993 you read a review of Ms. Homes's book in the *Washington Post* and called her in New York City?

What prompted you to call her on that day?

If Ms. Homes were not a successful, well-known figure, would you have ever called her?

You made a plan to meet in Washington several days later?

Was anyone else at the meeting? Was the meeting taped or otherwise recorded or monitored by anyone?

What was your reaction to meeting Ms. Homes?

When you met her, were you surprised by the degree to which she looks like you?

Does she look more like you than your other children?

Despite the physical similarity at that meeting, you asked Ms. Homes if she would consent to a paternity test—saying that you had no question as to the likelihood that she was your child, but that your wife was insisting, and that you would need that in order to be able to take her into your family. Is that correct?

What made you question Ms. Homes's paternity?

After the blood was drawn, as you were walking out with Ms. Homes you told her you had something you wanted to give her—and yet you didn't give her anything?

What did you want to give her?

Was it something of your mother's? A family heirloom?

Several months later, you phoned Ms. Homes to say you had the results of the test, and you asked Ms. Homes to once again meet you in a hotel in Maryland?

At that meeting you told Ms. Homes that you were in fact her father—that the DNA test said it was 99.9 percent likely—and you asked, "What are my responsibilities?"

What did you envision as your responsibilities?

What were your intentions toward Ms. Homes when you asked her to submit to the test?

Did you follow through by "taking her into your family"?

Before you discussed the results with Ms. Homes, did you discuss them with anyone else?

Did you discuss them with your wife?

Why did you not offer Ms. Homes a copy of the test result?

What did you do with the test result?

When did you give a copy to your lawyer?

Did you keep a copy for yourself?

Do you typically give the one and only copy of an important document to your attorney?

Did you not put it in your safe deposit box because you didn't want your wife to discover it?

But didn't you tell Ms. Homes that it was your wife who insisted on Ms. Homes's having the paternity test before you could "take her into your family"?

Was the reason your wife wanted Ms. Homes to have the DNA test that you had portrayed Ms. Ballman to your wife as a floozy to make it seem like you were Ms. Ballman's victim?

You arranged for your eldest son to meet Ms. Homes?

How did that meeting go?

Was your son happy to have more information about something that had only been a dim memory from his childhood—the time he spent with Ms. Ballman?

Was there a lot of tension in your home when your eldest son was a boy?

What was the occasion of your wife meeting Ms. Homes?

Is there a reason why your wife wouldn't like Ms. Homes?

Why did you say to Ms. Homes later that she and your wife didn't hit it off?

*   *   *

Did Ms. Homes ever ask you for anything?

Do you have concerns about Ms. Homes making a claim on your estate?

Did she ever in any way indicate that she had any interest in your estate?

Did you have her take the paternity test in order that you might by name exclude her from your estate?

When did you last speak to Ms. Ballman?

And what was the substance of that call?

Did you see Ms. Ballman in the months before she died?

Did your wife know you were meeting her?

How did she look? Was she still attractive?

Did Ms. Ballman ask you to ask Ms. Homes if she would give her a kidney?

And what did you tell Ms. Ballman?

Did you later tell Ms. Ballman that in fact you had asked Ms. Homes and that she said no?

Did it occur to you that Ms. Homes did not know about Ms. Ballman's condition, nor did she have a chance to say good-bye?

Did you go to your own personal doctor and inquire about donating a kidney to Ms. Ballman?

Did you tell Ms. Homes that you had done that?

And what would your wife have thought about that— would you have had the surgery without telling her?

Did you know that Ms. Ballman was going to die?

How did you feel when you heard that Ms. Ballman had passed?

And your last phone call with Ms. Homes—several months after Ms. Ballman's death—how did that go?

How did it end? Did you say, "Call me anytime. Call me in my car. My wife's not usually in the car"?

Why would Ms. Homes need to call you in the car as opposed to in your home?

Is anyone harming you, confining you, not allowing you to make and receive calls and/or mail?

Are you angry with Ms. Homes?

When Ms. Homes's New York lawyer called you—the same man who called you to tell you that Ms. Ballman had passed—and asked you for a copy of the DNA test, you told him never to call you again and referred him to your lawyer.

Mr. Glick called your lawyer and was told by your lawyer that the DNA document had been misplaced and that you would not sign an affidavit of paternity.

Did you know that Mr. Smith had misplaced the test results?

Are you concerned that other important documents may have been misplaced or mishandled?

Does it not seem a little too convenient that Ms. Homes is asking for this document, and now it is missing?

You have children and now grandchildren? Do they look like you, Mr. Hecht?

You have adopted grandchildren as well. Do they look like you also?

Do they have a right to know who they are—where they came from?

What is your understanding of why Ms. Homes wants this document?

If Ms. Homes is your biological relative, why should she not be treated in the same way as your other equally biological children are treated? Why should she have different, less than equal, rights?

Does that seem fair? Are you a fair man? A just man?

Could you please repeat for the record your name?

And Mr. Hecht, could you please for the record state the names of all your children?

My Grandmother's Table

Jon Homes, Jewel Rosenberg, and A.M. Homes

Jewel Rosenberg, my grandmother, my adoptive mother's mother, graceful, grandiloquent, profound. She is in some ways why or how this book exists. I am not sure that I would have become a writer if it weren't for her, nor would I have gone to such lengths to become a mother. Without Jewel Spitzer Rosenberg there would likely be no Juliet Spencer Homes—a girl who is now almost three, with no biological relation to my grandmother yet bearing a striking physical relation to her.

When the events charted in this book began to unfold, my grandmother was too old to make good sense of them and my mother elected not to tell her about the return of my biological parents. That decision bothered all of us—my grandmother was the ruler of the family, the queen bee; she was the one we went to about everything, the one with good advice, the one who was remarkable.

She was born in June of 1900, the turn of the twentieth century, in North Adams, Massachusetts. At fifteen she got glasses, looked up at the sky, and saw it wasn't all black—for the first time she realized there were stars. At sixteen, enrolled at North Adams Normal School (Massachusetts State College) and studying to be a teacher, she was called into the president's office and told she would never get a teaching job because she was a Jew. She didn't tell anyone about the incident—except her brother Charlie.

In my grandmother's house there was a table built in the year of my birth by the Japanese-American artisan George Nakashima from wood my grandmother selected at his shop in New Hope, Pennsylvania. The table is seven feet long, lush—French walnut. It is subtle, not announcing itself as something special until you spend time with it, until you get a feel for it. Then its significance becomes clear.

This was the family seat. This was where we gathered, where my grandmother, our matriarch, held court, where her brothers and sisters and their children and their children's children came to celebrate, to discuss, to mourn.

There have been great multigenerational political and philosophical debates at this table, especially when my

grandmother's brothers Charlie and Harold would visit—
the family radicals. They put themselves through college,
changed their name from Spitzer to Spencer, ostensibly to
protect the family from their radical reputations, but con-
veniently also hiding their Jewishness. They both studied
law but never practiced. Charlie went to work in a
Chicago steel mill and became a union organizer, and
Harold married the dancer Elfrede Mahler and went to
Cuba, where he taught English and she became the head
of Cuba's modern dance movement. When they came to
town, we would spend hours at the table, debating everything from the current political situation to the lyrics of
songs they made up as children.

This table was where my grandmother fed us. She had
long ago taught herself to prepare the traditional French
cuisine that my grandfather had grown up with—and had
long ago progressed from a Massachusetts farm girl to a
seriously sophisticated intellectual.

As a writer I think of narratives—family stories. Growing up, I was never sure about whether or not I could or
should absorb the family history. At family gatherings
great-aunts and -uncles from around the world would pull
their chairs in close and tell stories about life on my great-
grandparents' farm in North Adams, Massachusetts. I fell
in love with these stories, felt attached to them, but also
was made uncomfortable—this agreed-upon narrative was
not my narrative. "It's not my history, not my family," I

would whisper to my mother. "We are your family, believe me," my mother would say. I wanted to believe, but something felt off, inorganic.

Growing up, I had two adopted cousins who were black—they lived in upstate New York and we didn't see them all that often. Once when we were all at a relative's house for dinner—the adults downstairs, the three of us playing in the upstairs bedroom—I said, "I'm adopted too," trying to make a connection. The cousins looked at me blankly—"No you're not." "Yes I am." I was insulted that they didn't believe me—it didn't occur to me then that because I was white like my parents they thought I couldn't possibly be adopted. "Mom, am I adopted?" I yelled downstairs. "What are you children doing up there?" was the answer.

When she was in her late nineties I would visit my grandmother at her home outside of Washington every couple of weeks. We sat at the table and drank tea and talked. While we talked, she rubbed the table, her hand unconsciously moving in circles as if polishing the wood, repetitiously stroking it like a talisman, for comfort, for the giving and getting of wisdom.

We each sat in her familiar place, my grandmother at the head, I just to the left.

At her age, she was perhaps now even older than the

tree the table had come from—in my mind they are inexorably bound.

"We went up to the old farm," I said very loudly.

"You did? And you were able to find it?"

"Yes."

The weekend before, my cousin (also a writer) and I had driven up and down the hills of North Adams on an impromptu pilgrimage to find the farm where my grandmother grew up. The dirt driveway had long ago dissolved; the only way in was by foot. We climbed quickly, ascending into the mythology of the farm.

The original buildings remained, crumbling, collapsed, but still identifiable. I conjured images of my grandmother as a child, one of nine born to Lithuanian immigrants at the turn of the century on this Massachusetts dairy farm. I imagined her walking down the dirt road to a one-room schoolhouse, picking wild blueberries, helping my great-grandfather milk the cows and tend the chickens. I remembered her telling me the Mohawk Trail was just out the back door, and in my mind she was outside playing a real-life version of cowboys and Indians, substituting farmers for cowboys, cows and plows for horses and guns.

My cousin went on an ersatz archaeological dig, using a knife to poke in the dirt near one of the buildings. After a few minutes, he pulled out an old bottle.

"This must mean something," he said.

I nodded. We each took a couple of slate shingles from the crumbling roof and made our way back to the car.

"Tell me about the farm. How was it?" she asked, as if half expecting there was still someone there leading the cows out to pasture in the morning and back home again at night.

"Interesting." I told her about the landscape. She closed her eyes. I told her about the rolling hills, the tall trees, Mount Greylock in the distance.

"Just as I remembered it," she said.

She looked at her table. I imagined this table echoing something, some other great long farm table in my great-grandmother's country kitchen. I see my grandmother's nine brothers and sisters as children underfoot in their mother's kitchen. I see my great-uncles as teenagers in the summer selling buckets of water to overheated cars on the Mohawk Trail. I feel their grief when their fourteen-year-old sister, Helen, dies of diphtheria in 1912. I see their brother Maurice staying in North Adams—becoming the town doctor, delivering over twelve hundred babies.

My grandmother rubbed her finger along the grain of the wood.

Again, her hand circled the wood. "Tell me about you," my grandmother said.

"I'm fine, I've been working hard, I've been thinking

about buying a little house out on Long Island, a cabin where I can go and write."

She nodded. "It's important to have a house of your own," she said.

"Tell me about you," I said back to her.

"I've got nothing to tell," she said. "I'm bored."

She had worked her entire life—full-time until she was eighty-six. In 1918, two years before women won the right to vote, she came to Washington by herself, got a job in the War Department, and soon brought her brothers and sisters down from the farm. In 1922 she met my grandfather, the Romanian-French hatmaker, during a summer visit home when he happened to be working at his uncle's hat shop in nearby Pittsfield, Massachusetts. In the mid-1920s my grandfather sent for his younger brothers Julian and Maurice, hoping they would stay in America. The boys came for a summer but didn't like it—they couldn't get girlfriends because they didn't speak English. They returned to Paris and in the 1940s were deported from Paris to concentration camps—Julian to Drancy and then Auschwitz, and Maurice to Auschwitz. Neither survived.

Later, in Washington, D.C., my grandparents started a successful wine importing company, and when she was seventy-eight, Jewel Rosenberg became a founding director of the first bank in the United States organized by women for women.

Whatever I know about how to live my life, I learned from her. When I graduated from college and wanted to become a writer, she lent me the money to buy an IBM Selectric typewriter. I dutifully paid her back $50 a month, and when the debt was repaid, she wrote me a check for the entire amount. "I wanted you to know what it means to work for something."

Back at the table, she sighed. "I don't know what to do with myself. I don't feel useful anymore."

"It's your turn to rest and let others do things for you."

"I'm not a rester, I'm a worker."

"Let's go for a ride," I said, getting up from the table. We drove to a local farm, the place where my mother took me apple picking and pumpkin hunting as a child. I drove up a rutted road toward the berry patch.

"Where are we? This is beautiful, it reminds me of North Adams."

I parked beside a row of blueberry bushes and opened her door.

She made her way to the bushes and started grabbing at the berries and popping them into her mouth, her ninety-eight-year-old fingers suddenly nimble. Sweeping her hair back, she looked up at the sky and moved down the row, picking rapidly. She was a girl again, filling the basket with ripe, warm berries. "This is exactly how it used to be."

We drove home with the basket of berries on her lap. She squeezed my leg. "Buy your little house," she said, and I did.

I called her from the little house on Long Island. I stood in the small yard and told her what I was planting: rosebushes, tulip bulbs, seeds for carrots, beets, and squash. I had turned over a small square of land at the far end of the yard and began calling it "the field." I told her about tilling the field, tending my crop—the enormous satisfaction in this work, in being away from the city, my hands deep in the dirt.

She turned ninety-nine. "When are you coming home?" she asked several times in each conversation. "Soon," I told her. "Soon, I am coming home."

And then she was gone, the only person I've known to die unexpectedly at ninety-nine. I hurried back to Washington. I went to her house. I moved from room to room. I sat at the table, waiting. I had the feeling that she too felt she left too soon. She seemed to still be there, hovering, floating, packing.

I stayed for a while, just sitting, comforting myself with the echoes and objects that were like symbols, vessels of history.

At the end of the summer I pulled my carrots out of the ground, as proud of them as I was of any story or novel I'd written. She was the person I would most want to share them with; she was the one who would understand when I held up the green grassy ends and proudly said, Look what I made.

I see now that I am a product of each of my family narratives—some more than others. But in the end it is all four threads that twist and rub against one another, the fusion and friction combining to make me who and what I am. And not only am I a product of these four narratives— I am also influenced by another narrative; the story of what it is to be the adopted one, the chosen one, the outsider brought in. In the living room bookcase of my parents' house there was a two-volume slip-cased set called *The Adopted Family*. One of the volumes was a book to be read to the adopted child, and the other was a book for the parents. I would often sit with that book not sure entirely what it was about but sure that it was of great import, that in some way it was quite literally about me. I felt like a doll whose package comes along with a book.

As a child, I devoured biographies—in particular a set of biographies for children called *Childhood of Famous Americans*. I read each of them again and again; two in particular stuck in my mind: Eleanor Roosevelt and Babe Ruth. And at some point they conflated into a character of my own making, Eleanor Babe, a sort of early superhero— not only did she start organizations like Unicef, she had a mean curve ball. Thinking back on those two books, it's clear why they lodged in my thoughts; both Eleanor Roo-

sevelt and Babe Ruth were sent away by their families—
Eleanor to live in London with aunts who had no understanding of her, and Babe to a children's home in
Baltimore after his mother died. It was their outsider experience, their loneliness, that I identified with. They were
invisible adoption heroes—not only had they survived but
they succeeded.

It was the death of my grandmother that compelled me to
try to have a child of my own. Motherhood was something
that terrified me. I have a great fear of attachment and an
equally constant fear of loss—I am not sure if this is true
for everyone, but for me the ghost of the dead brother still
and always looms. When I was younger I always thought I
would adopt a child, but after Ellen's death and then my
grandmother's, I felt I wanted a biological child, and so it
was something that I decided to do. It had never occurred
to me that it would be difficult to get pregnant. I started at
thirty-nine, and in the end it took two years, thousands of
dollars, the best of medical science, and two miscarriages
before my daughter was born.

"What's the matter?" my mother asked. "Isn't adoption good enough for you?"

"Of course it's good enough," I said, but it wasn't
that—I felt compelled to try my hardest, to issue a biological echo, to see myself before myself, writ large and small
and as fully related as one can ever be.

*   *   *

Months after my grandmother had passed, my mother called and asked if I would like my grandmother's table.

"I know it's big and that your house is small, but I think it would be nice if you had it."

The table came in through the side door, carried by four men, carefully wrapped.

"These are tables of great weight," one of the men said, and he was right, but the weight was not so much literal as emotional. I inherited much more than an object—it was a mandate to live and work as hard and with as much grace and style as she did.

At first the table looked out of place, lost. I oiled it. I rubbed it with a soft cloth, moving my hands over the surface and noticing the richness of the tone—the lived-in marks that Nakashima called Kevinizing after his son Kevin. I thought of the spiritual life of the wood, what it gave beyond a surface.

The first time I used the table, I invited a friend over for lunch. I took my usual spot. Instead of looking at a painting on my grandmother's living room wall, I was now looking out a window at a bird feeder. I set two places at the table, hers and mine. My friend sat in my grandmother's place and something felt strange.

"I need to change places with you," I said.

The friend looked at me oddly—she didn't understand.

"Could we switch?" I asked, and then I slid into her seat.

When the table gets dry—thirsty—its surface looks pale, parched. I rub it with oil; it drinks and then glows. And while it is only a table, an object made of wood, it is a perfect and constant reminder of how to live, how to stay connected. It was in this little house—which I wouldn't have bought without my grandmother's nod and a gift that helped with the down payment—that I got the phone call from my mother saying my mother had died. It was in this house that I first miscarried and that, a year later, I celebrated my child's first Christmas and Hanukkah. It was in this house, at this table, that I sat alone unpacking the four boxes from my mother's house in New Jersey. It was this table that could hold those boxes.

The table is the centerpiece of our family life. It is where on the weekends my young family gathers—my daughter draws her pictures here; together we make cookies and decorate them. Each time I sit here I remember myself in my grandmother's kitchen, in awe and admiring her spice rack, her jars of cookie sprinkles and cinnamon hearts. Now, sitting in what was my grandmother's seat, I watch my daughter sitting in my spot to my left. I watch this girl, who more than anyone reminds me of my grandmother. She carries the same facial expressions, the same gestures, the same simultaneous compassion and judgment.

I witness the way she moves through her life, the confidence with which she carries herself. Like my grandmother, she takes great pleasure in making sure that others are taken care of. And as I am thinking this, she gets up from her spot, comes over, and gently pushes me out of my seat.

"I need your chair," she says, climbing up, filling the vacated spot.

I am my mother's child and I am my mother's child, I am my father's child and I am my father's child, and if that line is a little too much like Gertrude Stein, then I might be a little bit her child too. Most important, now I am Juliet's mother, and that brings with it a singularity of love and fear that I have never known before, and for that—and she is truly a blend of all four family lines—I thank all of my mothers and fathers, for she is my greatest gift.

Did I choose to be found? No. Do I regret it? No. I couldn't not know.

Acknowledgments

With great thanks: Phyllis R. Homes, Joseph M. Homes, Jon S. Homes, Edith Dugoff, Dan Gerstein, Belle Levin, Rita Ogren, Buddy Rosenberg, Marc H. Glick, Alison Smith, Amy Hempel, Patricia McCormick, Marie Sanford, Paul Slovak, Ellis Levine, Sarah Chalfant, Jin Auh and the staff at the Wylie Agency, Amy Gross, David Remnick, Deborah Treisman, Peter Canby and the staff of the *New Yorker*, Sara Holloway, Ian Jack and the staff at *Granta*, David Kuhn, Lanny Davis, Harvey Schweitzer, Brian Frosh, Elizabeth Samuels, Linda Reno, John Gray, Maria Dering, Alice Evans, Erin Markey, Michael Oster, Trent Duffy, Elizabeth MacDonald, Bliss Broyard, Mary Fitzpatrick, Betsy Sussler, Hilma Wolitzer, The Writers Room, Elaina Richardson, Candace Wait and the Corporation of Yaddo.